MEXICO

MAJOR WORLD NATIONS
MEXICO

Jack Rummel

CHELSEA HOUSE PUBLISHERS
Philadelphia

Chelsea House Publishers

Contributing Author: Jeff Beneke

Copyright © 1999 by Chelsea House Publishers,
a division of Main Line Book Co.

First Printing

1   3   5   7   9   8   6   4   2

Library of Congress Cataloging-in-Publication Data
Rummel, Jack.
Mexico / Jack Rummel
p. cm.—(Major world nations)
Summary: Surveys the history, topography, people, and culture of Mexico, with
emphasis on its current economy, industry, and place in the political world.
1. Mexico—Juvenile literature. [1. Mexico.] I. Title.
II. Series.
F1208.5.R86   1990   89-28261
972—dc20 CIP AC
ISBN 0-7910-4763-6

CONTENTS

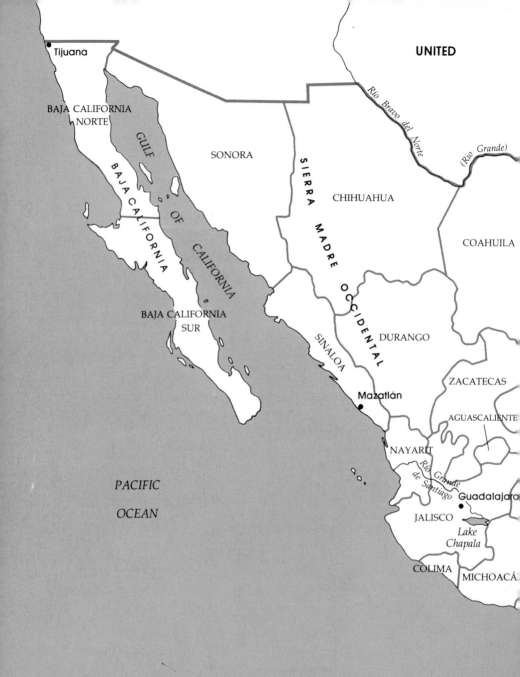

Tijuana

UNITED

BAJA CALIFORNIA
NORTE

GULF

SONORA

Río Bravo del Norte

(Río Grande)

BAJA CALIFORNIA

OF

CHIHUAHUA

COAHUILA

S
I
E
R
R
A

M
A
D
R
E

O
C
C
I
D
E
N
T
A
L

CALIFORNIA

BAJA CALIFORNIA
SUR

DURANGO

SINALOA

ZACATECAS

Mazatlán

AGUASCALIENTE

NAYARIT

Río Grande
de Santiago

PACIFIC

OCEAN

Guadalajara

JALISCO

*Lake
Chapala*

COLIMA MICHOACÁ

STATES

BERING
STRAIT

NORTH

AMERICA

ATLANTIC
OCEAN

PACIFIC
OCEAN

CENTRAL AMERICA

SOUTH

AMERICA

ATLANTIC

OCEAN

Monterrey

NUEVO
LEÓN

TAMAULIPAS

M A D R E   O R I E N T A L

AN LUIS
POTOSÍ

an Luis Potosí

NAJUATO

QUERÉTARO

HIDALGO

MÉXICO

Mexico
City

TLAXCALA

PUEBLA

MORELOS

GUERRERO

SIERRA   Acapulco

MADRE   DEL   SUR

VERACRUZ

Veracruz

GULF OF MEXICO

BAY OF
CAMPECHE

YUCATÁN

Chichén
Itzá

PENÍNSULA

QUINTANA

ROO

Cancún

YUCATÁN

CAMPECHE

TABASCO

Río Grijalva

Usumacinta

Río

OAXACA

CHIAPAS

BELIZE

GUATEMALA

GULF OF
TEHUANTEPEC

FACTS AT A GLANCE

Land and People

Area	761,830 square miles (1,980,758 square kilometers)
Highest Point	Mount Orizaba, 18,501 feet (5,606 meters)
Major Rivers	Río Grande de Santiago, Río Usumacinta, Río Grijalva, Río Bravo del Norte (Rio Grande)
Major Lakes	Lake Chapala, Falcon Reservoir
Capital	Mexico City (population 24 million)
Other Major Cities	Guadalajara (population 3.3 million), Monterrey (population 2.9 million), Puebla (population 1.2 million), Ciudad Juárez (population 1 million), Veracruz (population 328,000)
Population	96 million
Population Density	126 people per square mile (48 per square kilometer)
Official Language	Spanish
Ethnic Groups	Mestizo (mixed European and Native American descent), 60 percent; Native American, 30 percent; Criollo (European descent), 9 percent

| Religions | Catholic, 89 percent; Protestant, 6 percent; other, 5 percent |
| Average Life Expectancy | 70 years for men, 77 for women |

Economy

Resources	Oil, agricultural products, ores and minerals, natural gas
Exports	U.S. $96 billion: manufacturing (84%); petroleum and derivatives (10%); agriculture (5%); other (1%)
Major Industries	Oil and petrochemicals, steel, automobiles, fertilizers, tourism, food and beverages
Principal Trading Partners	United States, Europe, Japan, South America, Canada
Currency	Peso, divided into 100 centavos (approximately 7.9 pesos equaled U.S. $1 in 1997)
Average Gross Domestic Product	U.S. $3,900 per person

Government

Form of Government	Republic with two legislative houses (Senate and Chamber of Deputies)
Head of State	President (elected to one six-year term)
Elected Officials	President, 128 senators, 500 deputies, 31 governors, the mayor of the Federal District of Mexico City, and municipal officials
Administrative Organization	31 states, each with a governor, and the Federal District of Mexico City, ruled by the federal government; also municipal councils administered by mayors
Judiciary	Supreme Court divided into six subcourts

HISTORY AT A GLANCE

by 15,000 B.C.   The first Native American inhabitants arrive in Mexico.

5000 B.C.   The cultivation of corn is perfected.

3500 B.C.   Villages and towns appear in central Mexico.

1200–200 B.C.   Olmec civilization flourishes in the Gulf Coast region of Mexico.

A.D. 200–600   Teotihuacán civilization flourishes in the valley of Mexico.

300–900   Mayan civilization reaches its peak in the Yucatán Peninsula, the jungles of Chiapas, and the highlands of Guatemala and Honduras.

1250–1520   The Aztecs rule central Mexico, eventually controlling most of Mexico.

1520   Hernán Cortés conquers central Mexico and establishes Mexico City as the seat of the Spanish Empire in the New World.

1520–1810   Mexico, ruled by a Spanish viceroy, is organized into the Spanish colony of New Spain.

1810	Father Miguel Hidalgo y Costilla leads a revolt against the Spanish, which is crushed within months.
1821	Agustín de Iturbide leads another revolt against Spain, and this time Mexico wins its independence. Iturbide becomes the first emperor of Mexico a year later.
1821–61	Mexico is politically unstable.
1836	The Mexican province of Texas, inhabited by homesteaders from the United States, revolts and wins its independence from Mexico.
1846–48	Mexico loses about a third of its territory to the United States in the Mexican War.
1861	Benito Juárez becomes president of Mexico.
1863	The French invade Mexico to make Archduke Maximilian of Austria its emperor.
1867	Juárez triumphs over the French and resumes his presidency.
1877–1911	Porfirio Díaz rules Mexico.
1910	Francisco Madero calls for an uprising against the Díaz dictatorship.
1911	Díaz flees the country, and Madero is elected president.
1913	Madero is deposed and killed by General Victoriano Huerta.
July 1914	General Venustiano Carranza becomes president.
November 1914– January 1915	The troops of generals Francisco "Pancho" Villa and Emiliano Zapata occupy Mexico City.
1915–20	Carranza returns to rule but battles the forces of Villa and Zapata.
1919	Zapata is assassinated by the forces of Carranza.
1920	Carranza is assassinated by the forces of General Álvaro Obregón, who becomes

president of Mexico. The revolution ends, and the modern era in Mexico begins.

1921-33 The first postrevolution presidents establish economic and wage reforms.

1929 The Institutional Revolutionary party (PRI) is founded as the National Revolutionary party.

1934-40 President Lázaro Cárdenas nationalizes the oil industry and reorganizes the labor movement.

1968 The widening gap between the rich and the poor leads to a large student strike in Mexico City; the strike quickly turns into a riot.

1970s New oil reserves and rising prices make oil the most lucrative industry in Mexico.

1981 Mexico's currency, the peso, is devalued, from 26 to 45 pesos to the dollar, marking the beginning of a grave economic crisis in Mexico.

1985 A powerful earthquake rocks Mexico City, killing up to 20,000 people.

1988 Carlos Salinas de Gortari is elected president. Accusations of fraud lead to electoral reforms.

1994 The North American Free Trade Agreement (NAFTA) takes effect. An armed group known as the Zapatistas, protesting poverty and oppression of Native Americans, revolts in the state of Chiapas. The PRI's Ernesto Zedillo Ponce de León is elected president after the original PRI candidate is assassinated.

1995 Mexico receives a $51 billion emergency loan to stem its continuing debt crisis. Major scandals involving former president Salinas and other leading political figures weaken the PRI.

1997 Cuauhtémoc Cárdenas becomes the first elected mayor of Mexico City. The PRI loses its majority in the Chamber of Deputies.

*The remains of Chichén Itzá, in Yucatán state, are magnificent reminders of the ancient
Mayan culture, which flourished from the 4th through the 10th centuries.*

1

Mexico and the World

Mexico boasts the oldest civilization in the Americas. The first signs of settled town life occurred in the central valley of Mexico about 5,500 years ago. By the 8th century A.D., the Mayans, an ancient Native American civilization, had created a remarkably advanced system of astronomical science. In the 15th century, just before the Spanish conquered Mexico, the two largest cities in the world were probably Beijing, in China, and the Aztec capital Tenochtitlán, in central Mexico.

Mexicans take pride in their long and rich history. Yet they are also aware that their country is now facing some of its greatest challenges. The wealth that has come to Mexico from tourism and oil drilling has not resulted in a high standard of living for most of its citizens. Mexico's middle class is growing, but an uneven distribution of wealth has been a problem throughout the country's history and still plagues Mexico today. Today's generation of Mexicans must confront poverty, illiteracy, poor health care, unemployment, and a large foreign debt. Moreover, after years of dominance by a single political party, many Mexicans have developed a lack of confidence in their own political system.

The republic of Mexico occupies the southern part of North America, located between the United States on the north and Guatemala and Belize on the south. It has long coastlines on both its western and eastern sides. The Pacific Ocean on the west and the Gulf of Mexico and the Caribbean Sea on the east provide Mexico with access by water to the rest of the world, which is important for the export of oil. To the northwest, the Gulf of California (also called the Sea of Cortés) separates the Baja California peninsula from the Mexican mainland.

Mexico is the northernmost nation of Latin America, a region that acquired its name through the conquest and colonization by Spain and Portugal in the 16th century. The Spaniards and Portuguese brought to their new colonies their religion, customs, and languages, which are derived from Latin, the ancient language of the

Romans. The "Latin" habits and language of the Old World were transferred to the New. Thus the region came to be known as Latin America.

Mexicans are closely tied to their Latin American neighbors because they share a common language and heritage. But Mexico is also tied to the United States, emotionally and economically, for a number of reasons. There was a time when the southwest United States, including Texas, New Mexico, Arizona, California, Nevada, Utah, and Colorado, belonged to Mexico, and today hundreds of thousands of Mexican immigrants live in those states. Many Mexicans, seeing the wealth and dynamism of their northern neighbor, believe their country should adopt the same system of government, education, and work habits as the United States. At the same time, some Mexicans view the United States as an alien, commer-

Hundreds of Mexicans wait for nightfall and a chance to cross the border into the United States. A poor economy and an uneven distribution of wealth force thousands of Mexicans to emigrate, legally or illegally, every year.

cialized nation. These Mexicans are more cautious and fear that their traditional culture will be overpowered by American institutions and practices, and that in striving after prosperity, Mexican values will suffer.

For the most part, Mexico and the United States are friendly neighbors. They share a peaceful border of almost 2,000 miles (3,200 kilometers); they are major trading partners; and there is frequent contact between the two peoples. In the mid-1990s, about 15.5 million Americans and Canadians visited Mexico each year for work or pleasure, and 126,000 Mexicans emigrated to the United States each year.

Some problems do exist between the two countries. The U.S. government estimates that as much as half of the heroin and marijuana and most of the cocaine smuggled into the United States comes from or through Mexico. The Mexican government claims it is trying to wipe out narcotics trafficking in Mexico, but it also points out that if there were no demand for narcotics from the United States, the narcotics trade would not exist. Thus many Mexicans believe that drug addiction and trade are as much American as Mexican problems.

Illegal immigration of job-hungry Mexicans into the United States is another issue the two countries have not yet settled. Many Mexicans enter the United States either temporarily or permanently without proper permits; they are thus called illegal aliens or illegal immigrants and risk being deported (sent back to Mexico). Much of American agriculture, especially in the West, depends on seasonal laborers who journey north to the United States from Mexico. Quite a few industries also use Mexican laborers, who will work long hours at cheaper wages than most Americans—the threat of deportation leaves them in no position to bargain—because the wages are good by Mexican standards. From Mexico's point of view, illegal immigration mitigates its unemployment problems; laborers find work across the border, and the country benefits from the money they earn there and send back to their families. The United States also benefits; farmers, ranchers, manufacturers, and consumers profit from the exploitation of cheap Mexican labor. Illegal labor does, however, have its drawbacks. Illegal aliens take jobs that might otherwise go to U.S. workers, and Mexican laborers suffer from what are usually terrible working conditions, which they have no power to change. Although American employers are required to check the legal status of employees, 300,000 Mexicans enter the United States illegally each year.

Mexicans live in one of the most important and interesting countries in Latin America. Recent controversies about issues such as free trade, drug smuggling, and human rights have inspired a greater worldwide interest in the whole region. As Latin America's interaction with the world community grows, Mexico's role will become increasingly complex.

The Plaza de Armas, the oldest plaza in Mexico, marks the center of Veracruz, once Mexico's most important seaport.

2

Land of the Shaking Earth

Perhaps the best description of Mexico's physical geography was given by the Spanish conquistador Hernán Cortés. After conquering the Aztecs and claiming Mexico for the Spanish crown, Cortés returned to Spain in 1528. There, in the Spanish capital of Madrid, Charles V, Holy Roman Emperor and the Spanish monarch, asked him to describe the newly won territory. Cortés crumpled up a piece of parchment and laid it on the king's table. With this simple gesture he cleverly conveyed to the king the most striking geographical feature of Mexico: its rugged, mountainous terrain.

Mountains cover about 80 percent of Mexico. The great mountain ranges are known as the Sierra Madres, which means the "mother mountains." The Sierra Madres were formed hundreds of millions of years ago by volcanic action and the slow but continuous pressure exerted by moving pieces of the earth's crust. This process, which pushed the crust rock up into mountains, still continues. When these pieces of the earth's crust, called tectonic plates, scrape against each other, they jar the rock under the surface of the earth and cause earthquakes. Throughout its history, Mexico has been especially prone to earthquakes, such as the severe one that struck

Mexico City in 1985. The Aztecs called the country "the land of the shaking earth."

There are three great ranges of the Sierra Madres in Mexico: the Sierra Madre Oriental, Sierra Madre Occidental, and Sierra Madre del Sur. The mountains of the Sierra Madre Oriental, on the east side of the country, run parallel to the Gulf of Mexico from near the Texas border to south of Mexico City. Some of the tallest mountains in Mexico are found in this range. Many of these are the remains of inactive volcanos. This is the case with Mexico's two tallest mountains, Orizaba (18,501 feet or 5,606 meters), in Veracruz state, and Popocatepetl (17,930 feet or 5,433 meters), in Puebla state. Their snow-capped peaks can be seen from great distances.

The Sierra Madre Occidental, in the western part of the country, stretches 800 miles (1,280 kilometers) from the U.S. border almost to Mexico City. Canyons, some deeper and longer than the Grand Canyon of the United States, cut through this range.

The mountain range in the south of Mexico is called the Sierra Madre del Sur. They run along the Pacific coast from south of Mexico City to the Guatemalan border. Although these peaks are not high, they are especially rugged and have kept the western coast somewhat isolated for much of Mexico's history.

Ecology and Climate

The Sierra Madres both define and divide Mexico. Not only are they its most striking geographical feature but they exert a strong influence on the climate and ecology in all parts of the country.

Mexico has three basic climatic zones, which are determined by their relationship to the mountains. It is hot and humid in the low coastal areas along the southern Pacific coast and the southern Gulf of Mexico coast. There the temperature is usually hotter than 72 degrees Fahrenheit (22 degrees centigrade). The region receives between 60 and 140 inches (150 and 350 centimeters) of rain each year; the states of Tabasco and Chiapas may get as much as 200

The majestic, craggy cliffs of the Sierra Madre Oriental sweep across Nuevo León state. Broad-leafed agave plants appear in the foreground.

inches (500 centimeters) in a year. The area along the gulf is especially prone to hurricanes like the one that devastated the Yucatán Peninsula in 1988. Because it is so hot and humid, this tropical zone is called the *tierra caliente*, which means "hot land." Bananas, cacao beans (from which chocolate is made), rice, sugarcane, oranges, grapefruit, mangoes, chicle (which is used to make chewing gum), and rubber trees grow there. Some of the animals that live in the tierra caliente are armadillos, tapirs, monkeys, macaws, parrots, bats, crocodiles, iguanas, and snakes.

Inland, Mexico is drier and cooler. The northwestern areas, particularly the states of Chihuahua and Sonora and most of Baja California, are very dry, averaging less than 12 inches (30 centimeters) of rain a year. Yucca trees, agave cacti, and mesquite bushes grow in these arid regions. Lizards, coyotes, and wildcats live there. Closer to the mountains, where it is cooler but more humid, the increased rainfall supports pine and oak forests; corn and coffee are grown there. But because these areas are not generally good for farming, they are usually used for cattle ranching and mining. Because of its overall high elevation, the northern part of Mexico is colder than the rest of the country. It belongs to the climate zone called the *tierra fría*, which means "cold land." This zone also includes the high mountain peaks throughout the country.

In between the tierra fría and the tierra caliente is the *tierra templada*, or "temperate land." Most of Mexico, including Mexico City and most of the central Mexican plateau, has this climate. A moderate elevation (between 3,000 and 6,000 feet or 909 and 1,818 meters), temperatures of 60 to 70 degrees Fahrenheit (15 to 20 centigrade), and rainfall of 20 to 30 inches (50 to 75 centimeters) make the tierra templada especially suitable for agriculture. Wheat, potatoes, cherries, peaches, apples, and beans grow there. This climatic zone is home to a great number of animals also found in either North or South America, including ocelots, rabbits, skunks, bears, deer, and such birds as mockingbirds, parakeets, ducks, pelicans, sandpipers, turkeys, doves, and partridges.

Several major rivers wind through the country, and numerous lakes dot the terrain. Perhaps the best-known river is the Río Bravo del Norte, known in the United States as the Rio Grande, which provides a wide border between Mexico and the state of Texas. The Río Grijalva and the Río Usumacinta run through Chiapas and Tabasco states, meet, and then drain into the Gulf of Mexico. The Río Grande de Santiago is more dramatic, flowing west from the central plateau, contributing to Lake Chapala in Jalisco state, and continuing through a 430-foot (130-meter) waterfall at Juanacatlán near Guadalajara and miles of deep canyons before emptying into the Pacific Ocean. Of Mexico's lakes, the Chapala, in Jalisco state near the Pacific Ocean, is the largest at 650 square miles (1,690 square kilometers).

Mexico is a big country. It occupies approximately 762,000 square miles—almost a third the size of the 48 continental states of the United States, or roughly equal to the size of Western Europe minus Scandinavia. Its 32 separate states, each with a distinctive history and people, harbor a great diversity of climate, ecology, and terrain. Yet even though great diversity exists among the states, groups of them share enough similarities so that four regions stand out.

The Cradle of Mexican Civilization: Central Mexico

The central Mexico region is centered around the nation's capital, Mexico City, and extends several hundred miles in all directions. This is the heartland of the Mexican nation—the most populous part of the country and the site of the most important cities of the ancient Mexican Indians. Mexico City has always been at the center of Mexican civilization. Under the Aztecs, the city was known as Tenochtitlán. Before then, in a slightly different location, it was called Teotihuacán. Usually the tribe that ruled Mexico City was the strongest tribe in Mexico and controlled an empire that at times stretched from what is now Guatemala in the south to as far away as the U.S. border in the north. Ruins of these older cities can still be seen today in Mexico City.

Besides being the seat of the federal government, Mexico City is also the commercial and intellectual capital of Mexico. A majority of the country's major industries and its most important newspapers, magazines, and television stations are based here. With a population of 24 million people, it is a megalopolis, a monstrously large and sprawling city—the biggest urban area in the world. Mexico City has grown so large because the Mexican government

has lavished it with financial inducements to attract industry. And in spite of recent agricultural reforms and rural support programs, many peasants from the country are still drawn to the city in search of work. Through immigration from the countryside and the high birth rate, Mexico City gains an estimated 2,200 people every day—more than 800,000 new citizens every year. Despite terrible smog and high crime rates, the city's growth continues.

Guadalajara is another major city of the central Mexico region. With 3.3 million inhabitants, it is Mexico's second largest

Smog over downtown Mexico City points out one of the problems of being the largest urban center in the world.

city. The Río Grande de Santiago waters the fertile plains around Guadalajara, an area known for its farms and ranches. It was here, in the state of Jalisco, that the *charriada*, or Mexican rodeo, was created in the 18th century. It consisted of roping, horsemanship, and steer wrestling. Mexican cowboys later organized charriadas in the United States, where they eventually became known as rodeos.

Mexicans make tequila, an alcoholic beverage, from the blue agave cactus. This cactus grows only in the countryside near

Guadalajara. Tequila is the national liquor of Mexico. Considerable amounts of it are exported abroad, bringing in much-needed foreign currency.

The Gulf Coast

The Gulf Coast region of Mexico extends from near the Texas border to the Mexican state of Tabasco. Its major cities are port towns located directly on the Gulf of Mexico. Veracruz, with a population of 328,000, was founded by Cortés in 1519 and is the most

Guadalajara, Mexico's second largest city, is surrounded by mountains. Known for its gardens and mild climate, Guadalajara attracts visitors year round.

important town on the Gulf Coast. It was for many years the only port of entry into and out of New Spain, as Mexico was then called.

Oil and agriculture have made the Gulf Coast area richer than other areas of the countryside, although the wealth created by these two industries has not been shared equally among the people of the Gulf Coast. As in the rest of Mexico, a small percentage of very wealthy people control most of the money. But there has been enough wealth in the Gulf Coast area so that middle- and working-class people have benefited too. Many economists are predicting that the Gulf Coast, with its prosperous oil and agriculture base, will be a fast-growing region in the years to come.

The South: Land of the Native American

The southern part of Mexico, comprising the states of Oaxaca, Chiapas, Yucatán, Campeche, and Quintana Roo, is the Native American heartland of Mexico. Half of this area consists of mountains; the other half is covered with dense jungle. Oaxaca is the homeland of the Zapotec and Mixtec Indian tribes, and descendants of the ancient Mayas live in Yucatán and Chiapas.

This region is one of the poorest of Mexico. There is virtually no industry, and most of the people live on small farms, where families eke out a living by growing just enough food to feed themselves. Almost half of the people who live in this region do not know Spanish; they speak only their tribal dialects. Schooling and health care are rudimentary in many of these isolated jungle and mountain villages.

The state of Oaxaca gave Mexico two of its presidents: Benito Juárez, who drove out a French occupation army in the mid-1860s, and Porfirio Díaz, who was president of Mexico from 1877 to 1911. In spite of its national political history, Oaxaca remains resistant to control by the capital, Mexico City. The dominant tribe of Oaxaca, the Zapotecs, were never completely subjugated by the Aztecs, the central political power in Mexico before the Spanish, so there is a long history of local control of Oaxacan affairs.

The Yucatán Peninsula (the states of Yucatán, Campeche, and Quintana Roo) also resists the controlling hand of the federal government in Mexico City. The Mayas of the Yucatán, like the Zapotecs, were never conquered by the Aztecs, and during Spanish

Descendants of the Mayas, these Native Americans live and work in the isolated, rural villages of the Chiapas state. About 30 percent of the Mexican population is Native American.

colonial times, the Mayas and Spaniards who lived in the Yucatán had considerable leeway in running their state. The distance between Mexico City and the Yucatán also made it difficult for the national government to exert much control. In fact, until 1950, when a rail line from the capital opened, it was much easier for a resident of the Yucatán to travel to Havana, Cuba, than to Mexico City.

Traditionally the Mayas have been treated with either cruelty or indifference by the Spanish and their descendants. Not surprisingly, the Mayan regions have occasionally erupted in violent resentment. In 1849 the Mayas rebelled against Mexicans of Spanish blood (known as *criollos*) and their mixed-blood allies (known as mestizos). The rebellion lasted three years, and the state of Yucatán remained in chaos for decades thereafter. In January 1994, Native America groups from Chiapas formed the Zapatista Army of National Liberation and led an armed revolt against the central government.

The North and Baja California

The north is one of the most dynamic and industrialized parts of Mexico. Monterrey is a city of 2.9 million people in the northeast, about 200 miles (320 kilometers) from the Gulf of Mexico and Brownsville, Texas. Monterrey is the most industrialized city of the area with its steel mills, chemical factories, and car plants. During the 1970s, the United States and Mexico passed new laws encouraging the growth of factories in towns on the border, such as Ciudad Juárez and Tijuana. In these factories, called *maquiladoras*, foreign companies set up assembly plants where laborers take imported raw materials and finish them for export. In 1994, Mexico, Canada, and the United States signed the North American Free Trade Agreement (NAFTA), designed to eliminate gradually all tariffs among the three countries. Encouraged by NAFTA, many American businesses have relocated operations to northern Mexico or expanded existing facilities there. As a result, the area has been growing faster than any other section of the country.

The Baja California peninsula, separated from the rest of Mexico by the Gulf of California, is an arid, mountainous finger of land running north-south between the Pacific Ocean and the Gulf of California. Except for the extreme north, where maquiladoras attract laborers from the whole country, the Baja Peninsula is very sparsely populated. Divided into two states, Baja California Norte and Baja California Sur, the peninsula is mostly desert, with less than 10 inches (25 centimeters) of rainfall a year. Some parts of the peninsula have no recorded rainfall at all. Cactus, scrub oak, and pine make up most of the vegetation; the elephant tree also found there grows nowhere else in the world.

Cotton, grown in the north, is the most important crop in the region, but the maquiladoras are the biggest economic factors there. They are responsible for turning Mexicali, Tijuana, Ensenada, and Tecate into boomtowns.

The Olmecs, Mexico's first great civilization, carved giant heads like this one (actually a plaster reproduction) out of stones quarried at least 80 miles (128 kilometers) away.

3

The Eagle and the Serpent

Before Cortés arrived in 1519, there were no people of European or African descent living anywhere in the Americas. Most of the people were racially and culturally quite different from those found today in Mexico. These people are known as Native Americans because they were the Western Hemisphere's original inhabitants. They were organized into a large number of tribal groups, each of which could be identified by a distinctive style of clothing, the language it spoke, the art and architecture it made, and the gods it worshiped.

The Native American peoples migrated approximately 30,000 years ago from northern Asia to the North American continent by way of a land passage (now covered by the waters of the Bering Strait) between Alaska and Siberia. Gradually these different groups drifted south. Archaeological evidence suggests that the first Native Americans arrived in the central valley of Mexico at least 15,000 years ago.

For thousands of years these early tribes lived by hunting animals and gathering wild plants, but the food supply eventually became inadequate for a growing population. The first Mexicans had to develop agricultural techniques to support their communities. The most important staple crop developed in Mexico was maize, or corn. Maize was domesticated from its wild variety into a hearty and reliable food crop in central Mexico around 5000 B.C. By 1200 B.C. the technique of cultivation was sufficiently advanced that for the first time enough surplus food was produced to free small numbers of people from hunting and farming. Thus castes of hereditary rulers, priests, artists, and craftsmen gathered in the first cities of the Americas and developed a distinctive culture.

The Olmecs

The Olmecs were the first great pre-Columbian civilization in Mexico (pre-Columbian means that they existed before Columbus came to the New World). They settled the coastal lowlands along the Gulf of Mexico in an area not too far from the present-day city of Veracruz. Much of the terrain is covered in dense jungle and swamp. Whereas the central highlands had supported one maize crop each year, the tierra caliente of Veracruz offered a climate that supported cultivation of two crops a year. The abundance of food allowed the Olmec culture to grow and become strong.

Olmec cities appeared around 1200 B.C. During the next 400 years Olmec cities were built in the Gulf Coast lowlands and as far away as the Pacific Coast in what is now the state of Guerrero.

Unlike the Greeks and Chinese, the Olmecs left no written record of their history. Everything we know about them has been constructed from physical evidence left in the ruins of their cities, the largest of which are found at La Venta in the state of Veracruz and San Lorenzo in the state of Puebla.

Because of the size of its ruins and the astonishing number of artworks found within its domain, it is apparent that La Venta was the largest Olmec city. It was probably the capital of the Olmec Empire. Situated on a three-acre island that rises out of a river, La

This illustration from a Mayan codex depicts a corn harvest. Pre-Columbian Mexico domesticated corn, also called maize, around 5,000 B.C.

Venta is one of the strangest and most perplexing ruins in Mexico. Sometime around 1000 B.C., the Olmecs built a 100-foot-high (30-meter-high), cone-shaped temple and numerous other stone buildings and public spaces there.

Olmec artists also carved enormous heads that rose from the earth at numerous places in the city. The heads are made out of basalt rock, which is not found in the area of La Venta. Archaeologists have discovered that the Olmecs quarried the rock for the heads and other art and construction projects from sites at least 80 miles (128 kilometers) away and shipped the stone to their capital by barge, an undertaking that called for considerable energy and sophistication. These huge heads, many of which are as large as 8 feet high by 6 feet wide (2.5 by 2 meters) and weigh as much as 55,000 pounds (24,750 kilograms), are sculpted with the greatest of skill. The heads probably represent Olmec gods, such as the jaguar god, which is thought to have been the supreme Olmec deity.

Archaeologists also discovered a ceremonial ball court at La Venta. Most Native American cultures throughout Mexico's pre-Columbian history shared a great passion for a ball game that was a cross between basketball, soccer, and Roller Derby. The object of

Players in this ball court at the Temple of Jaguars were expected to get a solid rubber ball through the high hoop without using their hands.

the game was to maneuver a large rubber ball, probably slightly smaller than a present-day basketball, through a stone hoop that projected from one of the sloping walls of the court. The ball could not be touched with the hands, and as it was made of solid rubber it was very heavy, so scoring a goal proved to be difficult. Ball courts are prominently featured in all the ruined cities of ancient Mexico, and apparently ball players held a position of considerable prestige. The court was a place of ceremony and suspense, and spectators often gambled on the outcome of the game. It is also thought that the game was a kind of ceremony that held great religious significance. The losing team, composed of three to five members, was sometimes sacrificed after the game; the athletes would either be decapitated or have their hearts ripped out by priests in an effort to placate the gods and to assure the orderly progress of human life in what was seen as a chaotic world. This ball game was still being played when Cortés arrived in Mexico in 1519, and he brought two teams of players back with him to Spain in 1528 to perform for the Spanish royal court.

Archaeological evidence shows that the Olmec civilization came to an end around 200 B.C. No Olmec cities or works of art and architecture from later dates have been found. Nobody knows the exact reason for the collapse of this brilliant culture; tribes from the central plateau might have invaded the Olmec people, or their food supply might have become too small to support their growing population.

The Mayas

The Mayas were the next major city-building civilization to appear in Mexico. They occupied a large territory in the scrubland of the Yucatán Peninsula, the jungles of the Mexican state of Chiapas, and the highlands of Guatemala and Honduras. The Mayas came onto the scene around A.D. 300, and their civilization flourished until about A.D. 900. The Mayas appear to have worshiped many of the same gods that the Olmecs revered, and there is much evidence that the Olmecs had a profound influence on the Mayas. Like the Olmecs, the Mayas excelled in architecture and art. They also perfected advanced systems of astronomy and mathematics, and they left a detailed record of their religious practices and mythology. We know much more about the Mayas than we do about the Olmecs because the Mayas left written communications carved in stone columns called stelas and written in parchment paper books called codices. We also have records of Mayan life that the Spanish wrote shortly after their conquest of Mexico.

Like all of the other Native American groups of Mexico, the Mayas were polytheists, which means they worshiped many gods. Three of these gods, however, seem to have more importance than the rest. These are Chac (the god of rain), Ah Kin (the sun god), and Itzam (perhaps the supreme or ruling god). These three were frequently carved into Mayan buildings and stelas. Chac was sometimes depicted with a human head and a long elephantlike snout for a nose, and sometimes with deep-set eyes and fangs because he was believed to have evolved from a snake. Ah Kin, the sun god, is frequently associated with the jaguar, which was a sign of royalty and the priesthood. Usually Ah Kin is shown with what look like goggles over his eyes, a T-shaped incision on his forehead, crossed eyes, and scrolls curling out of his mouth. Itzam is depicted as a giant reptile that is part alligator, part iguana, and part serpent. It is thought that Itzam is the god most directly associated with the Mayan king, and for this reason he may have been the god of wisdom and perhaps of war.

The Mayas have left tantalizing fragments of text that allow us to understand how they saw the world and the universe. They believed the world was a precarious place ruled by unpredictable gods capable of ending life at any moment. Only a strict adherence to religious practices would please the gods and bring personal good fortune as well as the continued existence of the world itself.

Chac, the Mayan rain god, appears here in human form, but he is sometimes depicted as a snake.

Thus the Mayas constantly studied nature (especially the skies) and practiced religious rituals in order to determine the various moods of their gods. Like all the major Mexican Native American civilizations, they performed ritual human sacrifices to appease angry or unresponsive gods. The Spanish chronicles tell of thousands of sacrifices made in the Aztec capital of Tenochtitlán, and archaeological evidence points to regular human sacrifices in the Mayan city of Chichén Itzá. One sacrifice involved throwing a person into a well, called a cenote, at dawn. If the victim was still alive by noon he or she was rescued, because this meant the person had been spared by the rain god Chac and had been sent back to earth with a prophetic message.

The Mayas developed extraordinarily accurate tables of astronomical observation. They measured time by these observations and developed a mathematical system that included the concept of zero, which was found in few other ancient cultures. Their primary unit of time was the katún, which was composed of 20 years. Thirteen katúns made a complete cycle of time (260 years). The Mayas feared the end of a 260-year cycle because the world might come to an end at such a time. Like the Olmec, the Mayan civilization disappeared quickly and mysteriously. No great building projects appear after the year A.D. 900, and although the people of the Mayan Empire did not disappear, they seem to have fallen to a less advanced standard of living. It is thought that the Mayas, who had developed sophisticated techniques of farming in the jungles, exhausted the soil's ability to produce food, causing famine and perhaps revolt among the common people.

The Aztecs

The last great pre-Columbian civilization in Mexico, the Aztec, was originally a wandering tribe that lived in the northern part of Mexico.

Cultures as rich and sophisticated as those of the Olmecs and the Mayas had already risen in the central Mexican valley before the time of the Aztec Empire. Around A.D. 200 one of these cultures, the Teotihuacán people, constructed the first great city in the valley of Mexico. This city was also called Teotihuacán, and by A.D. 500 it had become a metropolis of more than 100,000 people. Along with

Constantinople in Turkey and Beijing in China, it ranked as one of the great cities of the world during that era. (By way of contrast, Rome was a small city of perhaps 50,000 people in A.D. 500.) But when the Aztecs first appeared in the valley of Mexico, the Teotihuacán people were long gone; many other tribes had won and lost control of the valley since the high point of Teotihuacán civilization.

Aztec legend tells of how the Aztecs wandered for years in the deserts of Chichimeca, in the north. They worshiped a god called Huitzilopochti, who was represented by a hummingbird. According to Aztec myth, this hummingbird god would lead them to a small island in a lake where an eagle perched atop a cactus was eating a snake. The Aztecs actually found such a place around 1250: an island in Lake Texcoco, a now dry lake just northeast of Mexico City, on which they eventually built a great city called Tenochtitlán. In 1250 the dominant tribes of the valley were the Culhuacan and the Tepanec, for whom the Aztecs served as mercenaries. The Aztecs remained a subservient tribe for approximately 150 years, but by 1430 they had become masters of all of the peoples living in the valley of Mexico.

During the next 90 years the Aztecs managed to extend their empire over much of Mexico. In the process they built Tenochtitlán, which was even more impressive than Teotihuacán had been. By the time of the Spanish invasion of Mexico in 1519, the Aztec capital of Tenochtitlán was in effect the capital of all of Mexico. Two hundred thousand people lived on the island of Tenochtitlán. Another 400,000 lived in communities within a 15-mile (24-kilometer) radius of the capital. In all approximately 1.2 million people lived in the 68-by-50-mile (109-by-80-kilometer) oval that is the valley of Mexico. This vast population declined after the Spanish invasion and was not equaled again until the early part of the 20th century.

The god Huitzilopochti reigned supreme in Tenochtitlán. The Aztecs built a pyramid temple in his honor and made an estimated 10,000 to 20,000 human sacrifices to him and to other deities each year. Unlike the Mayas, the Aztecs almost always sacrificed a victim by cutting open the chest and cutting out the still-throbbing heart, which was then placed in the mouth of a hummingbird statue. On certain special occasions, such as the 1487 inauguration of the new temple dedicated to Huitzilopochti and the rain god Tlaloc, the Aztecs sacrificed as many as 50,000 men, mostly captured warriors of enemy tribes, in a bloody 4-day religious carnival.

Human sacrifice on such a large scale tended to intimidate the tribes under Aztec control and ensured that no one rebelled against

the Aztec Empire. It also meant that the Aztecs enjoyed little real loyalty from the enslaved tribes. Such brutality would help the Spanish gain important Native American allies in their war against the Aztecs.

In the later years of his reign, the Aztec emperor Montezuma, a fearful and indecisive man who had ruled since 1502, became obsessed with a prophecy that foretold the end of the Aztec Empire by the appearance of a god named Quetzalcoatl (known as the plumed serpent god and usually represented in sculpture as a winged rattlesnake). Quetzalcoatl was a god who represented peace and culture for many of the tribes who had been conquered by the Aztecs. Because the Aztecs had conquered these other tribes,

A reconstruction of Tenochtitlán, including the great temple, depicts what this Aztec city might have looked like in its prime.

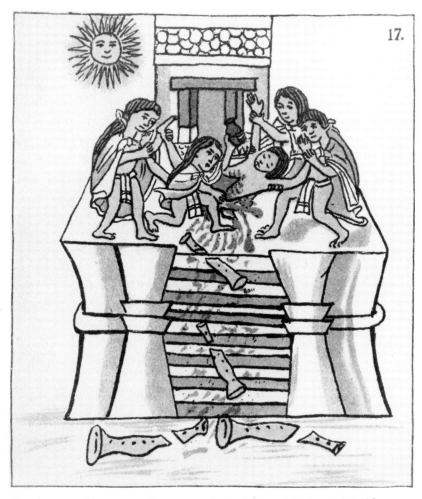

Four Aztecs sacrifice a captured enemy warrior by ripping out his heart. Ritual human sacrifice was common to all the powerful pre-Columbian civilizations.

it was assumed that their god, Huitzilopochti, had defeated Quetzalcoatl. Yet stories circulated among the defeated tribes that Quetzalcoatl would reappear someday to destroy the Aztecs and their hated hummingbird god. The exact form Quetzalcoatl would assume on his reappearance was unknown. When a Spanish expedition led by Francisco Hernández de Córdova appeared in the

Yucatán in 1517—strange, bearded, pale-faced aliens in winged ships who came out of the ocean riding strange animals and carrying metal shafts that spit fire—Montezuma thought it meant the end of his reign. The Spaniards had landed with horses and cannons and engaged in a few brief fights with Mayans before they boarded their ships again and returned to the Spanish base in Cuba. The Native Americans of Mexico did not know about cannons and gunpowder and had never seen horses or even cows. They assumed that the Spanish were gods, and that their leader was Quetzalcoatl.

Emiliano Zapata fought for peasants' rights in Morelos state and became one of the major figures in the revolution of 1910.

4

Conquest and Revolution

On Holy Thursday, April 21, 1519, a Spanish fleet led by Hernán Cortés anchored off the coast of Mexico near the place that would later become the city of Veracruz. Cortés's was the third expedition to be sent out from the Spanish bastion of Cuba to Mexico. News of Mexico's spectacular wealth returned to Cuba with the crews of the two earlier expeditions. Montezuma had presented bracelets, rings, and necklaces made of precious stones, gold, and silver to these men, hoping this would satisfy them, but the gifts only whetted Spanish greed and ambition. So whereas the leaders of the first two voyages had merely conducted exploratory missions, Cortés came to Mexico with cannons, horses, a 2-month supply of food, and 650 men, determined to conquer a new land for himself.

Cortés was fortunate enough to be aided by a Spaniard who had been captured by the Mayas on an earlier expedition to Mexico. This man had learned the Mayan language and something of the customs of the Native American people. Later Cortés luckily happened upon a woman, christened Marina, who spoke both Mayan and Nahuatl, which was the language of the Aztecs. With Marina translating Nahuatl into Mayan for the Spaniard who understood

49

Mayan, Cortés was able to speak to and understand the Aztecs, but they still had no way of knowing who he was or where he came from.

Soon after he landed in Veracruz, Cortés gained the allegiance of the major coastal tribe, called the Totonacs, who had been brutally treated by the Aztecs. The Totonacs, along with other tribes nearer the Aztec capital, had been forced to give a percentage of their sons and daughters to the Aztecs as slaves and sacrificial victims; they were also required to send tribute payment in the form of crops, silver, and gold. Naturally these tribes were eager to put an end to the Aztec Empire.

Cortés intimidated his crew into following him. When a group of his men tried to steal one of Cortés's boats and head back for Cuba, the commander severely punished the mutineers. Two were hanged, one had his feet chopped off, and the rest were whipped. Then Cortés ordered all his boats burned, so that no one could escape. His crew had no choice but to follow their commander into battle.

The march on the Aztec capital began on August 16, 1519. A dangerous and complicated game of trickery and double-crossing had arisen between Cortés and the Aztec ruler Montezuma. Cortés wanted to march peacefully into the Aztec capital of Tenochtitlán by pretending to be a friend of the Aztecs. Once there, he planned to defeat the Aztecs with a surprise attack. The Aztecs, in their turn, feared the Spanish and hoped that they would be defeated by a tribe called the Tlaxcalans. When the Tlaxcalans instead become allies of the Spanish, Montezuma felt he had no choice but to invite the Spanish as his guests into the Aztec capital.

The Spanish were astonished by what they saw in Tenochtitlán. The city was gleaming white. All the buildings, from the largest villas to the most humble adobes, were whitewashed with lime. All kinds of strange trees grew along the streets and next to the canals.

Atlivetsyan.

Cortés met with the Tlaxcalans and made them his allies against the Aztecs. The interpreter is probably Marina, a Mayan woman who spoke the Aztec language.

Tenochtitlán proved to be a garden city, a paradise of the kind that many of them had read about in medieval European tales of adventure and chivalry. Believing the arrival of Cortés and his troops to be the return of Quetzalcoatl, Montezuma gave the Spanish commander and his men the best living quarters and held banquets in their honor.

When Cortés realized that Montezuma was giving him the whole Aztec Empire without a battle, he immediately took advantage of the situation and imprisoned the emperor in the Spanish quarters.

He then ordered the temple of Huitzilopochtli to be converted into a shrine to the Virgin Mary.

Cortés heard that another Spanish expedition had landed on the Gulf Coast, and he left Tenochtitlán in order to keep these rivals away from his new paradise. When he returned to the capital, he discovered that his men had massacred the Aztec nobles during his absence and that an angry mob of Aztec soldiers had the Spanish surrounded. Cortés and his men, fighting their way out of the city, barely escaped to their allies, the Tlaxcalans. Montezuma was stabbed to death by either the Spanish or his own men, who were angered by his weakness.

Cortés enlisted the help of the Tlaxcalan Indians against the Aztecs. The Tlaxcalans, who had periodically served as Aztec slaves, were valuable allies.

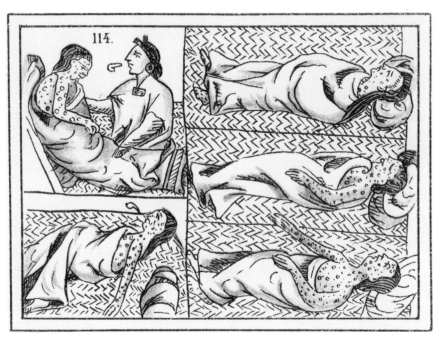

The Spanish brought new diseases to Mexico, such as cholera and smallpox. Because the people had no natural immunity, these diseases decimated the Native American population.

During the next five months the Spanish and the Tlaxcalans strengthened their forces. In the meantime, in Tenochtitlán, the Aztecs were falling to a secret Spanish ally: smallpox. Smallpox had been a devastating disease in Europe for many centuries, but by the 16th century most Europeans had developed tolerance enough to prevent it from wiping out whole groups of people. This illness was completely new to the Americas, however, and the Native American peoples had no natural defenses against it. Without even knowing it, the Spanish carried smallpox into Tenochtitlán. When the epidemic hit, its results were catastrophic.

While smallpox ravaged the Aztecs, Cortés's army of 20,000 Spaniards and Tlaxcalans attacked Tenochtitlán in an eight-month siege. They seized all the fertile land around the city and cut off the

Eighteenth-century Mexico had a flourishing Spanish elite that sought to combine New World wealth with European style and culture.

Aztec food supply. Eventually they stormed the city and captured the last Aztec emperor, Cuauhtémoc. The Spaniards encouraged the Tlaxcalans to take their revenge on the Aztecs; the Tlaxcalans slaughtered every man, woman, or child they found. By the time the Spanish reasserted control over the city, only a third of the inhabitants of Tenochtitlán were still alive.

Colonial Period and the War of Independence

The Spanish conquered the rest of Mexico and Central America swiftly. By 1550 all of Mexico was securely under Spanish control. Again disease, especially smallpox, aided the Spanish effort by dramatically weakening the strength of the opposing tribes. Estimates place the number of Native Americans in Mexico at the time of the conquest at approximately 20 million; 100 years later this number had dropped to only 1.2 million, a drop in population of nearly 95 percent.

The villainy of the early Spanish adventurers, or conquistadores, was well known in Spain, where they were often regarded as desperadoes, rebels, and murderers. They saw the Americas as a land where there were riches for the taking, so they plundered what they could in Mexico and then usually returned to Spain to retire in luxury.

During the colonial era these adventurers established many living and working conditions that still affect the country today. The principal inheritance from the the first colonists is the extreme exploitation of the poor by the rich. The Spanish set up a system of land ownership called the *encomienda* that gave huge tracts of land to the conquistadores and other favored Spanish immigrants. The Native American people who lived within the boundaries of these estates became, in effect, the slaves of the Spanish owners. This system lasted in one form or another for the entire 300 years of Spanish colonial rule of Mexico. It set up two basic classes in Mexico: at the top, the very rich, a tiny minority who controlled virtually all of Mexico's wealth, and at the bottom, the very poor, the vast majority who owned little or nothing and who could never expect to gain any material advancement.

During the colonial period the Spanish and the Native American populations began to mix through intermarriage, so that by the time of Mexico's independence from Spain most people in Mexico were neither purely Spanish nor purely Native American. These people, known as mestizos, over time became a new majority; neither Aztecs, Mayas, nor Spanish, they were the first Mexicans.

By the beginning of the 1800s, the Mexican people had developed a strong sense of national identity. Following the examples of the North Americans who had rebelled against the English and of the French who had thrown off their king, they wanted to establish their own nation, independent of Spanish rule.

The first mutiny against Spain, led by a radical priest named Miguel Hidalgo y Costilla, erupted in 1810. On September 16, Hidalgo issued a proclamation calling for Mexican independence (this day is now celebrated as one of Mexico's two independence days). Following the banners of the Virgin of Guadalupe, Hidalgo's troops began an advance on Mexico City. They took and massacred the Spanish garrison in the town of Guanajuato (north of Mexico City) but were defeated by a much smaller Spanish garrison at the gates of Mexico City. In 1817 Hidalgo was captured, defrocked, executed by a firing squad, and decapitated. For a decade his head hung in a cage at the scene of the massacre of the Spanish garrison in Guanajuato.

The struggle for independence continued in the countryside. Agustín de Iturbide, a commander of one of the Spanish militias in Mexico, finally defeated the Spanish in 1821. He betrayed the Spanish viceroy, seized Mexico City, and proclaimed himself emperor in 1822. His reign was short and disastrous; only 10 months after his coronation he was deposed by a group of rival military officers and forced to flee the country.

The next 40 years were a nightmare for Mexico. Presidents and governments came and went in quick succession as one after the other was deposed by military force. The most prominent politician of this era was Antonio López de Santa Anna, who served as president of Mexico 11 times. It was under Santa Anna that Mexico lost almost half of its territory to the United States in the 1836 Texas Revolution and between 1846 and 1848 in the Mexican War.

Two remarkable politicians restored order after this chaotic period. The first was Benito Juárez, a Native American of the Zapotec tribe from the state of Oaxaca who became president of the republic in 1861. Juárez was a liberal who sought to remove the influence of the Catholic church from government decisions and who favored land-reform measures that helped many of the poor peasants of the countryside. Juárez remained president in Mexico

City until 1863; he was forced to flee the capital with his government when the French invaded to establish Archduke Maximilian of Austria as emperor of Mexico. Juárez fought a guerrilla war against the French for four years, and in 1867 he finally prevailed. He returned to Mexico City and resumed his presidency, which lasted until his death in 1872.

After Juárez's death another politician from Oaxaca became president. This man, Porfirio Díaz, would rule longer than any other Mexican president. His dictatorial regime lasted 34 years, from 1877 to 1911. Díaz tolerated no opposition, and he frequently jailed opposition politicians. Under his harsh rule Mexico achieved remarkable economic and political stability at the price of political freedom. Díaz was determined to modernize Mexico. He invited American and British companies to build railroads and telephone

The Battle of Buena Vista was a turning point in Mexico's 1846–48 war with the United States. Mexico lost nearly a third of its territory as a result of this war.

lines, electric power plants, and steel mills in Mexico, but he did nothing to ensure a stable and prosperous nation after he gave up power.

Revolution of 1910

In 1907, President Díaz announced that he would not run for office again, but he quickly changed his mind when he saw other politicians positioning themselves to run for his office. In the end, Díaz did run again, and with the help of massive voting fraud he won the election.

President Porfirio Díaz was the virtual dictator of Mexico for 34 years. He stabilized the country but ruled with an iron hand. Protests against his method of governing led to the revolution of 1910.

His one opponent was Francisco Madero. The son of a wealthy family from northern Mexico, Madero was an unusual man for his time in Mexico. Thirty-seven years old, he was a spiritualist who did not smoke or drink and espoused vegetarianism. In a country where nearly everyone who could afford to do so ate meat, and where drinking was considered a sign of machismo, or manliness, it seemed unlikely that Madero would defeat the old president. Yet his obvious sincerity and integrity won the public's confidence. By June 1910 he was attracting large crowds. Díaz became so worried about Madero that he ordered his arrest several days before the election. Madero managed to escape and fled to San Antonio, Texas, where he called for a national uprising against Díaz in November 1910.

The call for revolution ignited the long-suffering Mexican people. In southern Mexico a peasant farmer named Emiliano Zapata formed a guerrilla band and gained control of most of the state of Morelos, and in the north Madero's army, which seemed to have sprung out of nowhere, easily routed Díaz's lazy and corrupt federal army. By June 1911, Porfirio Díaz had fled Mexico for Europe. He never returned.

From 1910 to 1920, Mexico was engulfed in the most troubled period of its very turbulent history. For 10 years it endured a violent revolution and civil war that left more than a million people dead and several million more wounded and homeless. At the beginning it seemed that the political conflict would end quickly. Francisco Madero was elected president after Porfirio Díaz fled, but his reign lasted only a year and a half. In February 1913 he was deposed by Victoriano Huerta, one of his own generals, and later executed. This military coup set off yet another round of fighting between rival generals. Pancho Villa, who had been one of Madero's key generals, defeated the more conservative generals who held power in Mexico City. By July 1914, Villa, Álvaro Obregón, and Venustiano Carranza

had retaken Mexico City for the revolutionary forces. This revolutionary victory too quickly dissolved into bickering among the winning generals. Carranza and Obregón sided against Villa and Zapata, but the latter two took control in November 1914.

The fiercest battles of the revolution were fought from 1914 to 1919. Villa was defeated and subdued by Obregón in two bloody battles in 1915. Zapata was ambushed and murdered in 1919, and his guerrilla war sputtered to a halt without his leadership. Finally, in 1920, Obregón turned against Carranza, defeated his forces in battle, and killed him.

Pancho Villa, one of the major figures of the revolution of 1910, sometimes allowed Hollywood to film his battles.

In September 1920, Álvaro Obregón became president of Mexico. In order to prevent a repetition of the power struggle that had occurred during the previous 10 years, he organized the political party that still rules Mexico. At first it was known as the National Revolutionary party, but it was later renamed the Institutional Revolutionary party (commonly known in Mexico today as PRI). With the creation of the PRI, the violent passions that had torn the country apart came to an end. The revolution of 1910, which one writer has called Mexico's "death feast," was over. Modern Mexico had been born.

Modern Mexico

The new leaders of Mexico wanted to establish social equality. They had plans for land and labor reform and a system of national education. Between 1921 and 1933, Mexico's presidents made great progress toward these goals, which slowed only during the Great Depression of the 1930s.

During the first years of the "Northern Dynasty," so called because the presidents of this period came from northern Mexico, the government built 3,000 new schools throughout the country. It took away 11 million acres (4.2 million hectares) from the great *latifundistas* (major landowners) and distributed them in hundreds of poor villages. It allowed workers to form a national labor union, which quickly attracted nearly 2 million members.

After a short period of more cautious development in the mid-1930s, President Lázaro Cárdenas came into office. His administration was marked by a revolutionary zeal not seen before or since in Mexico. President Cárdenas redistributed an additional 49 million acres (20 million hectares) of land and reorganized the labor movement. In one of the most popular moves in Mexican history, he nationalized the foreign-owned oil companies—that is, he passed a law that transferred ownership of the companies to the Mexican government. This gave Mexico a large share of the profits made from the export of Mexican oil.

World War II cut off many imports, and the Mexican government was determined to provide for itself. Agrarian and labor reform gave way to new business loans and tax incentives to encourage rapid industrialization. Mexico put its efforts into developing dams and highways as well as steel and petrochemical products.

The nation prospered, but government corruption throughout the 1950s, 1960s, and 1970s resulted in a widening of the rift between the rich and the poor. In the late 1960s high unemployment and inflation created great unrest. Guerrilla and terrorist activity, including kidnapping, became a problem; there were clashes between citizens and government forces. When students in Mexico City demonstrated against the government in 1968, federal troops were ordered to disperse them. Hundreds died in the riot that followed.

In the 1970s the discovery of new oil reserves and rising oil prices turned the economy around. Oil exporting became Mexico's biggest industry. Tourism also contributed an ever-increasing share to the national income. Encouraged by the economic boom, the Mexican government borrowed billions of dollars from foreign nations to pay for ambitious new development projects, but the early 1980s saw a collapse in oil prices along with an oil glut, and the Mexican economy fell once again.

An earthquake hit Mexico City in 1985, killing as many as 20,000 people and leaving 300,000 without homes. It devastated the area

The 1985 earthquake in Mexico City left 25,000 children homeless.

A man washes coffee beans in the southern state of Chiapas. Low prices for coffee added to the economic woes in Chiapas that helped prompt the Zapatista revolt.

and effectively ruined the tourist industry for a time. The debt crisis made it difficult for the Mexican government to rebuild quickly or to offer adequate aid. To make matters worse, corrupt government officials pocketed and misspent relief money.

During the 1980s, wars in Central America created new problems for Mexico, including refugees from El Salvador and Guatemala. Meanwhile, the Mexican government attempted to deal with the economic crisis through a number of reforms, some of them required by strict conditions placed on international loans to Mexico. Under President Miguel de la Madrid (1982–88), the government revoked protectionist measures, privatized many government-owned industries, and sharply cut public spending. But domestic and foreign debt still rose, and wages fell dramatically.

With the elections of 1988, the PRI's 60-year dominance began to falter. Carlos Salinas de Gortari, Mexico's finance minister and the PRI's presidential candidate, was considered by many to be partly responsible for the country's economic difficulties. Opposition parties on the left combined behind Cuauhtémoc Cárdenas, a former PRI member, whose father had been president in the 1930s. Amid widespread complaints of fraud, Salinas won the election, but the PRI lost seats in the Senate.

Salinas took office promising to do something about the national debt, electoral fraud, corruption, and poverty. Although the economy grew at a modest rate, inflation erased many of the benefits. Much of the economic growth was spurred by foreign investment, which rose because of Mexico's participation in the General Agreement on Tariffs and Trade (GATT) and NAFTA.

In January 1994, Native American groups from the state of Chiapas staged an armed rebellion, demanding social and economic changes. They called themselves the Zapatista Army of National Liberation, after the hero of the Mexican revolution Emiliano Zapata. After brief fighting, the government announced a ceasefire, and the two sides began negotiations that continued through the following years.

The 1994 election season was also disturbed by the assassination, in March, of the PRI candidate, Luis Donaldo Colosio. The PRI's replacement, Ernesto Zedillo, won the election, defeating both a conservative challenger from the National Action party and Cárdenas, who represented the new Democratic Revolutionary party. Still, the PRI's grip on power was loosening.

In the 1997 elections, the PRI lost its absolute majority in the Chamber of Deputies, and Cárdenas became the first elected mayor of Mexico City. Zedillo faced the task of leading an increasingly democratic but fragmented country into the 21st century.

Peasant women in the Mexico City marketplace still weave according to traditional methods.

5

The Mexicans

Mexico today is an ethnically diverse nation of 96 million people. In the five centuries since the Spanish conquest, many of the Native Americans and European immigrants (most of whom came from Spain) have intermarried to form a mixed people, the mestizos. This group is the largest ethnic bloc in the country. Calculations of the percentage of mestizos in Mexico today range from 55 percent to 76 percent or higher. A reasonable estimate is that mestizos make up about 60 percent of the population.

Another important ethnic group is formed by people of European descent, often called criollos (a term originally used to mean descendants of the Spanish conquerors). Though these people account for only about 9 percent of the Mexican population, they exert influence far beyond their numbers. In some cities, such as Mexico City, Monterrey, Puebla, and Guadalajara, the criollos own most of the businesses and industries and thus exercise great influence over the economy. Though many Mexicans take pride in their ethnically mixed heritage, the country is not entirely free of racial discrimination, which tends to favor criollos at the expense of mestizos and particularly of Native Americans.

Native Americans form Mexico's third important ethnic group, accounting for about 30 percent of the population. They belong to 56 officially recognized tribes. Many of these people do not know any Spanish and can speak only their native language. Most are poor and live in the countryside. They are likely to receive the least education and have the shortest life expectancy of any of Mexico's ethnic groups.

Social Classes

In terms of social classes, the Mexican people are divided into three basic groups: a small group of very wealthy citizens who control most of the financial resources of the country; a slightly larger but still relatively small middle class made up of teachers, businessmen, clerical workers, and professionals, such as lawyers, engineers, and doctors; and the vast majority of extremely poor people who own little or nothing.

Approximately 50 percent of the population lives in poverty. Mexico's largest cities are surrounded by enormous slums, with people living in shacks made of corrugated tin, cardboard, and broken cinder blocks. They have no running water, and open ditches serve as sewers. They do not receive money when they are unemployed, and although the government has raised literacy rates and opened training institutes, many Mexicans work only as occasional laborers or scavengers.

By contrast, the rich of Mexico live opulently. Many own two or three homes, often a main home in Mexico City and a villa in the coastal resort of Acapulco or in Cuernavaca, a vacation town in the mountains near Mexico City.

Mexico's annual gross domestic product per person (that is, the total production of the economy divided by the number of people) is U.S. $3,911 a year. Of course, most working-class and poor fami-

A small but growing set, Mexico's middle class tries to find a balance between economic security and its mestizo heritage. This woman owns a zapatería, or shoe store.

lies make far less than this. Even the middle class, which has been growing since the 1950s, has been particularly hard hit by the uneven economy, which has undercut many of its gains.

Dress and Food

Most Mexicans dress like people do in other modern, Westernized nations. Men, especially those who live in the cities, wear suits and ties; women wear dresses, skirts, and blouses; and the young wear jeans.

Many Native Americans, however, still wear the dress of their ancestors. The Mayas, for instance, often dress in plain, baggy, unbleached white cotton trousers and simple white cotton shirts. Many Native American women wear the rebozo, a type of shawl, and the huipil, a rectangular dress with openings for the arms and head. Hand woven and dyed with bright colors, the huipils are often decorated with images of plants and animals that are significant to the various tribes.

Workingmen, especially those who live in the country, wear a type of cape called the poncho that offers protection from the cold and rain. It also doubles as a blanket at night and is especially useful for sleeping in the open countryside. Men also wear hats known as sombreros. Some have wide brims; those worn by Native Americans are slightly upturned with a small tassel hanging from the back. The vaqueros, or cowboys, of the north wear wide-brimmed straw sombreros that are similar to the cowboy hats of the western United States.

Corn is still, as it was during the days of the Mayas, Aztecs, and Olmecs, the staple food of most Mexicans. It is eaten in various forms. One of these is the tortilla, which is a flat pancake made from cornmeal and water. It is often cooked in oil and used to wrap beans or chicken. Cornmeal is also an ingredient of the *tamal*. Meat cooked in a hot sauce is rolled in the meal, wrapped in corn shucks, and heated over a fire.

The other staple food of Mexico is the frijol, or bean. Beans come in many varieties and are often eaten with rice and hot peppers. One of the favorite Mexican frijoles is the pinto bean; another is the black bean. The *guajalote* or turkey, a bird native to the Americas, is a Mexican delicacy; Mexicans eat them during holidays with mole, a delicious sauce made of cocoa and several different kinds of dried chili peppers.

Religion

The Roman Catholic church has been the predominant religious force in Mexico throughout its post-Columbian history, as it has been for all Latin America. As long as the Spanish ruled Mexico, Catholicism was the country's official religion. Although independence from Spain in 1821 eroded the Catholic church's political prominence, it remained very powerful. The revolution of 1910, shaped by socialist and Marxist ideas, separated church and state definitively. In the 1920s, Catholicism found itself under attack because it was seen as a force that stood in the way of modernization; during that decade churches were destroyed, and many members of the clergy were harassed. Today ecclesiastical influence is generally accepted, and most Mexicans consider themselves to be Catholics.

Approximately half of Mexico's people live in poverty. In the outskirts of Mexico's cities, garbage scavengers look for any item they can salvage or sell.

A Yucatán woman prepares corn dough for tortillas. Corn and beans are the staple foods of the Mexican diet.

Religious Mexicans, particularly the Native American peoples, worship the Virgin of Guadalupe. In 1531 a Native American named Juan Diego is said to have witnessed the Virgin Mary walking on a hillside outside of Mexico City. This happened at the former site of a temple devoted to an Aztec goddess, and the leaders of the Mexican Catholic church, recognizing that Native Americans would accept Christianity more readily if it absorbed elements of their old religions, agreed to accept as fact the appearance of the Virgin. Shortly after, they built a church shrine at the site. Today it is one of the most important holy places in Mexico.

Men and Women

Mexico has a long-standing tradition of male dominance within the family, which is mirrored by society. Machismo is nurtured in boys, who are taught to be aggressive with their peers and assertive with women. As adults, they are expected to go out into the world, whereas women are relegated to stereotypical gender roles in the home.

Though macho attitudes have meant secondary status for Mexican women, the situation is changing slowly. Women were given the right to vote in 1953. In 1975 an equal rights amendment, which is largely unenforced, was added to the Mexican constitution. Women increasingly run for public office, and in recent elections have filled as many as 10 percent of the seats in the Chamber of Deputies. In addition, women have served as governors of states, have held posts in presidential cabinets, and have run for president. Among educated women, employment outside the home in nontraditional roles is on the rise. But most women still complete fewer years of school than men, are still tied to the home, and are not encouraged to study for professions at colleges and universities.

Native American and European religions combined to form a distinct Mexican hybrid. Here, dancers in Aztec costume celebrate the Mexican Catholic holiday of the Virgin of Guadalupe. This celebration lasts three days.

6

The Fiesta of Life

Every year Mexicans enjoy a number of celebrations and holidays that mark important religious and civil events. These holidays are called fiestas, and they are a cross between carnivals and holidays. Most fiestas last from one to three days. Usually they are held outdoors, typically in the plaza at the center of town, and feature food, fireworks, and carnival rides. In the evenings bands play music for dancing, and spectators watch the *castillo*, an elaborate fireworks display.

Many fiestas are religious in nature. Their origins may be traced to both Christianity and the earlier native religions. The Aztecs and other Native American groups staged religious fiestas throughout the year to beseech the gods for rain or ask for the birth of children. Even some of the symbols used by the Native American groups and the Christian church were similar. For instance, the cross was a widely used symbol in ancient Mexico. For the Native American people it represented the four directions of the universe. Because it was already such an important symbol, Native Americans easily accepted the idea of worshiping the Christian cross, even if they understood its meaning somewhat differently than the Christian missionaries who had been sent from Spain to convert them.

Mariachi bands are distinctively Mexican, entertaining tourists as well as providing dance music for patron saint day festivals.

The early religions have clearly influenced many of the Christian fiestas held today. This is the case with the festival of the Virgin of Guadalupe, the single most important fiesta in Mexico, held on December 12 to commemorate the 16th-century sighting in Mexico of the mother of Jesus. The Virgin of Guadalupe is in many ways similar to the Aztec goddess Tonantzin, who was considered to be the mother of all the Aztec gods. Tonantzin, like Mary, is considered to be a virgin. And also like the Virgin of Guadalupe, Tonantzin possessed the qualities of forgiveness and mercy.

The fiesta of the Virgin of Guadalupe is a national holiday. Many Mexicans make pilgrimages from their villages to pray at the shrine, and it is not uncommon to see men and women showing their devotion to the Virgin by crawling on their knees up the avenue that leads to it. The celebration usually begins on the evening of December 11, and although this is a serious religious holiday, the atmosphere is festive. Vendors line the streets around the church; dancers perform the traditional Native American dances of their villages; and a Ferris wheel offers rides a block away. The eating, dancing, and drinking usually last all night long. The next day a formal mass is held inside the church, and throughout the day worshipers enter the shrine to pray and offer thanks to the Virgin in the form of small tin or silver objects (called *milagros*, which means "miracles") shaped like hearts, arms, or legs, which are pinned to the walls of the cathedral near the statue of the Virgin to signify the giver's thanks for a cure.

Among the other important fiestas are two celebrations of Mexican independence, one in May that commemorates the defeat of French forces in a battle on May 5, 1862, and one on September 16 held in honor of the revolution of 1910 begun by Father Hidalgo y Costilla; the Three Kings Day on January 6, when people exchange presents among family and friends in imitation of the gifts presented to the baby Jesus by the three Magi; and the Day of the Dead on November 2, which honors spirits, particularly of ancestors.

Also every city, town, and village in Mexico holds a special fiesta in honor of its own patron saint. These take place on the the saint's birthday, so local fiestas occur all over Mexico throughout the year. Those celebrations are similar to the major ones, like that honoring the Virgin of Guadalupe, in that fireworks are shot off, food and drink are available, dancing is common, and the festivities last well into the night. But local fiestas call attention to the different customs of the various regions of Mexico. For instance, in the town of Papantlan in the state of Veracruz, a fiesta is held on Corpus Christi (the Thursday after Trinity in late May or early June) that features young men of the village dressed like bird gods, swinging from a long pole in the center of the town. This festival celebrates both Christ and the ancient sun-god of local residents. The performance is unique to that particular part of Mexico.

Visual Art

Beginning with the exquisite work of the Olmecs, Mayas, and Aztecs, Mexico has a rich artistic tradition. After the Spanish conquest, this tradition continued in the construction of churches and in the development of a new folk art that was a fusion of the old Native American traditions and the newer Spanish ones.

The 16th and 17th centuries were the high point of church building in Mexico. During that time all of Mexico's most famous churches were constructed. They reflect the merging of Native American and Spanish talents. Spaniards designed the churches according to the baroque and rococo styles of the era, but Native Americans built them and executed the carvings and paintings they contain. Baroque and rococo are intricate styles that use curved forms and include elaborate decorations, both on the inside and outside of buildings. This ornamentation calls for much intricate stone and wood carving and the use of great detail in fashioning objects out of gold and metal. One of the best-known Mexican churches is the Church of Santo Domingo in the city of Oaxaca. Built in the late 1500s, only a half century after the Spanish conquest, it is considered by many to be one of the most magnificent examples of baroque architecture in the world. Inside are 11 different chapels, decorated with angels carved in limestone and painted gold.

Although church art and architecture was the official art of Mexico, folk art was just as important, and Mexico is rich in this type of work. Much Mexican folk art is ceramic. The talavera dinnerware and tiles of Puebla are typical. Painted in bright primary or secondary colors, they use geometric patterns or depict scenes of Mexican village life. The black pottery of the town of San Bartolo near Oaxaca is also famous for its instantly recognizable style. All this pottery is covered in a smoky, black glaze. The potters of San Bartolo make plates and bowls as well as figures of guitar-playing mermaids and angel candlesticks. Perhaps the most typically Mexican folk art pottery is that of the Metepec people, who live near the town of Toluca in the state of Mexico. The Metepecs fashion bizarre and humorous scenes out of ceramic clay and paint

A potter displays his talent in Oaxaca.

them vividly in hot pink and lime green. These scenes often depict a skeleton figure, who represents Death, riding a motorcycle or sitting down with a family to eat at the fiesta. In this way, the idea of death, with which the Mexicans seem to be especially preoccupied, is personified and shown to be a part of life.

Mexican art reached a high point in the early part of the 20th century. During the 1920s and 1930s the artists Diego Rivera, David Siqueiros, and José Orozco adopted and became identified with the medium of mural painting—both outside and inside buildings. Rivera especially is known for mural art. He chose it as his major form of expression because it is a type of Mexican folk art. Mexican artisans and village painters had long depicted scenes of village life on public walls. Rivera employed this tradition on a grand scale and incorporated images from Mexican folk art (such as the death scenes of the Metepec potters) in his own work. By 1940 this style had become world famous and enormously influential in Mexico. Many of Rivera's scenes showed poor people fighting against rich landlords and priests. The revolutionary Mexican government that emerged from the revolution of 1910 approved of this kind of art; in time, Rivera received most of his financial support from the state. Later he was criticized by those who thought he had become a paid mouthpiece for the government. Nonetheless his work remains one of the most important contributions to Mexican visual art in the 20th century. His work can be seen in the halls of the National Palace and on the walls of the National University, both in Mexico City.

Literature

Mexican literature also has a long and brilliant past. It dates all the way back to the pre-Columbian civilizations. Once, whole libraries existed in Tenochtitlán, Oaxaca, and the Yucatán, but the Spanish destroyed most of these during the conquest. Intolerant of other people's beliefs, they considered the Native American writing to be

(continued on page 89)

82

Overleaf:
Mexico's terrain varies from barren deserts to tropical
jungles. Michoacán state, on the southwest Pacific
coast, is somewhere in between. A fertile region,
Michoacán is known for its corn, beans, chili peppers,
watermelons, and cantaloupes.

Mérida, in Yucatán, became one of Mexico's fastest
growing cities because of improved transportation.

The Yucatán has a high con-
centration of Mayan Indians,
who live in relatively under-
developed areas.

Sprawling Mexico City extends farther
into the central plateau every year.

Peasant farmers in rural areas have little access to modern agricultural methods, and communal farms have developed to relieve the heavy workloads.

Industry is slowly making its way into the Mayan communities.

Fishing is an important industry for exported goods. Shrimps, oysters, sardines, and giant perch get sold abroad, primarily to the United States.

These men wear white to stay cool while preparing for the Sunday market.

Children dress up to celebrate their town's patron saint day.

A weaver in Cuetzalán, Veracruz, with her family around her, works out of her home.

Children play outside their home in a Mexico City shantytown.

(continued from page 80)

ignorant and anti-Christian. Their destruction of these writings deprived us of much knowledge about life in pre-Columbian Mexico.

In fact, pre-Columbian libraries stored much more than religious texts. Works cataloging medicinal herbs, detailing tax and land-ownership records, and explaining Native American myths were stored as well. A few of these works, known as codices, still exist. The largest collection of codices, the Codex Borgia, was seized from the Mixtecs by the Spanish in the 16th century and was rediscovered in a Roman home in 1750 when a Catholic bishop rescued it from a child who was trying to set it on fire.

The *Chilam Balam of Chumayel*, a long narrative poem, describes the Mayan myth of the creation of the world. The Mayas did not claim to know how the earth and universe came into being, but they attributed its creation to a god or gods. The Mayas believed that the world was carried on the back of a turtle swimming through an immense lake. They further believed that all things were given a limited amount of time in the universe, at the end of which the person, animal, god, king, world, or thing would cease to exist. This lends a certain tragedy to the poetry in the *Chilam Balam*.

One of Mexico's finest poets lived in the colonial era, some 100 years after the conquest. Her name was Juana Iñez de la Cruz. She began her career as a lady in waiting to the wife of the Spanish viceroy in Mexico, but her social and literary success caused trouble, and she was forced to become a nun and retreat to a convent in Mexico City. There she wrote many of her most famous poems. Some of these were mystical rhapsodies about the nature of love. Others were meditations about science and defenses of her right to publish her work. Because women were not expected to engage in intellectual debate in 17th-century Mexico, Juana Iñez de la Cruz was finally silenced. She lived in solitude, deprived of her library and forbidden to write, for the last 10 years of her life.

This mural by Diego Rivera depicts a postrevolution official distributing land to the peasants.

The 20th century became another fertile period for Mexican literature. The revolution of 1910 prompted several novelists to examine the violence and injustice of this period of Mexico's history. Mariano Azuela's best-known book, *The Underdogs*, and Martin Luis Guzmán's two novels, *The Eagle and the Serpent* and *The Shadow of the Caudillo*, all deal with the period of the revolution.

In 1990, Octavio Paz, a poet and essayist, became the first Mexican writer to be awarded the Nobel Prize for literature. His best-known work is *The Labyrinth of Solitude*, a collection of essays exploring Mexican culture and life.

Carlos Fuentes, another internationally known Mexican writer, explores a contemporary Mexico troubled by changing relationships between the sexes and by the use and misuse of power. Two of his foremost novels are *The Death of Artemio Cruz* and *Where the Air Is Clear*. His book *The Old Gringo* has been made into a movie. Something of an international ambassador of Mexican culture, he has made the concerns and complexities of his country familiar to many readers all over the world.

Bales of fique fiber come from the tough threads of the agave plant.

7

Economy

At the time of the Spanish conquest, the vast majority of Mexican Native Americans were peasants who labored long, hard hours with little material reward. These people had no say in deciding who ruled them or how the goods they produced were distributed. An immensely rich elite at the top of society lived on the labor of the poor, and constant warfare, human sacrifice, and widespread slavery were facts of life for almost every tribe. Nonetheless, the standard of living of the Aztecs, Mayas, Totonacs, Tarascans, Mixtecs, and other tribes had at least attained a level of subsistence. The average family might not have had a varied diet, but its members generally had enough to eat, and although their dwelling place was simple, they had a place to live.

These basic economic conditions were the result of the tight, cohesive social structure of the tribes. Among the Aztecs and the others, everyone knew his or her place. After the Spanish conquest, the tightly knit social organization began to disintegrate, and the result was greater confusion and harsher poverty than had existed before the conquest. Mexico still lives with the legacy of this disorder today. It still has a small, immensely rich elite at the top of the social structure; but instead of widespread peasant slavery, it has runaway unemployment and homelessness.

Contemporary Mexico is an economically developing country; that is, its level of industrial production and standard of living are low when compared to fully industrialized countries, but greater than those of poorer nations. In Latin America, however, where development has lagged, Mexico is seen as a great economic success. Between 1940 and 1997, its economic growth increased by an average of five percent a year, making it one of the most dynamic economies in the region. Its manufacturing industries grew tremendously during this period, and for the first time in its history a relatively large middle class emerged as a significant part of the economy. An emerging middle class is generally seen as a positive development in a country because it points to a more stable economy. Mexico's middle class lives for the most part in the cities, and the wages its members earn from their jobs are spent mostly on goods produced in Mexico, helping to spur the economy.

Over the years, most economic incentives offered by the government have been targeted at urban areas, because the government has sought to encourage industrial, not agricultural, development. Today, agriculture, including forestry and fishing, employs 28 percent of the working population but accounts for only 7 percent of economic production. In the 1990s, the government did begin a program of land reforms, modernization, and subsidies to renew the agricultural sector. Still, rural people have seen relatively little rise in their standard of living, and they continue a long-term exodus to the cities, especially Mexico City, where many are forced to live in shantytown slums.

Economic History

For more than 300 years after the conquest, Mexico's economy was based on mining and on the cultivation of several export crops. The commodity that accounted for most of Mexico's wealth during this

For 300 years silver mining was the mainstay of the Mexican economy. Indians and mestizos alike suffered from terrible working conditions and did not share in the profits.

period—and its main export to the rest of the world—was silver. The first large silver mines exploited by the Spanish in Mexico were located in the state of Zacatecas, an arid region in north central Mexico some 350 miles (560 kilometers) from Mexico City.

Mexican silver had a great effect on Europe's economy. In 1500, before silver from Mexico entered its market, Europe had approximately 20,000 tons of precious metal circulating as money. By 1650 this figure had doubled, mostly because of the Mexican silver that came to Spain as taxes and payments for European luxury items such as wine, olive oil, cutlery, glassware, furniture, and paper.

Mexican silver also had an impact in Asia because of the trade from China through the Philippines (which was then a Spanish colony) to the Mexican Pacific coast town of Acapulco. Each year, Spanish ships brought Asian silks, pearls, velvets, satins, and spices to Mexico, where they were exchanged for Mexican silver coins.

Mexico began raising sugarcane for export in the early 19th century. Today, Mexico is a large exporter of processed sugar.

This trade became so profitable for the Chinese that in many places along the China coast Mexican silver coins became the preferred currency.

By the early 1800s, Mexico exported sugar, cotton, and coffee, which were grown in central and southern Mexico. All other economic activities produced goods that were consumed inside of Mexico. Agriculture, the biggest sector of the economy, produced beef and wheat for the cities along with the ever-present corn, squash, and beans.

Most land was held by a small number of powerful landlords, many of whom owned pieces of real estate as big as the smaller European countries; the Terrazas family, for example, owned several ranches in the northern state of Chihuahua, each as large as Belgium. These landlords owned not only land but whole villages and towns as well, and everyone who lived within their domain was in some way obligated to them.

At that same time, the majority of Mexicans, living in the countryside, were engaged in self-sufficient agriculture, called subsistence farming. They raised just enough to feed themselves and their families by growing a little corn, beans, and squash on their milpa, or small homestead. They did not have enough land, cash, or machinery to raise more than this.

During the late 1800s and early 1900s, Mexico began to industrialize, opening steel plants in Mexico City and Monterrey. Textile mills, cement plants, and fertilizer factories soon followed. The Mexican government has favored industry since the revolution of 1910, and industry now accounts for 29 percent of Mexico's gross domestic product (GDP), while agriculture accounts for 7 percent.

Since 1950, industrialization has been especially rapid. During this time, the government has lured many foreign investors with financial incentives, such as low taxes on businesses. Since 1994, the elimination of tariffs under NAFTA has further encouraged foreign investment, which rose from $449 million in 1940 to $1 billion in 1960, $2.8 billion in 1970, and $8 billion in 1996.

Foreign firms have long had a major presence in markets for automobiles, rubber tires, electrical appliances, food processing, and pharmaceuticals. Most of these firms are American, although Japanese and European companies are also active in Mexico, and their share of total foreign investment is growing.

Until recently, the Mexican government owned most of the country's basic industries, including banking, oil, steel, electrical production, petrochemicals, and communications. Since 1982, the gov-

The richest landowners lived in haciendas such as this one, with its big, open courtyard. These estates were so large that by 1910, 96 percent of Mexico's rural families were without land and had to live and work on the haciendas.

ernment has privatized most of its holdings, and it has changed many of the rules that made foreign investment in these industries difficult or impossible.

The tourist trade brings in nearly $6 billion each year, accounting for 5 percent of Mexico's GDP. Most tourists come from the United States and Canada, although there are some Europeans and Japanese as well. They cross over the border into Tijuana or fly to luxury resort cities such as Acapulco on the Pacific coast and Cancún off the Yucatán Peninsula. Others visit the ancient ruins in and around Mexico City or farther south in Oaxaca, Chiapas, and the Yucatán. More recently, tourists have begun to explore the largely deserted state of Baja California Sur. However, natural disasters in the 1980s and 1990s caused extensive damage to Mexico City, Cancún, and Acapulco, resulting in temporary declines in tourist income.

Oil and Foreign Aid

Just as silver was the cornerstone of the Mexican economy during the colonial period, oil has been its driving force since the 1970s. Oil was discovered in Mexico in the early years of the 20th century, but Mexico did not become a large exporter of the commodity until the mid-1970s.

In May 1972, in the humid marshlands of the Gulf Coast, the Mexican national oil company, called Pemex, discovered an enormous reservoir of oil and natural gas near the city of Villahermosa. Soon other oil fields were located, both on the land and offshore in the shallow waters of the gulf. Estimates of petroleum reserves skyrocketed from 6.3 billion barrels in 1975 to 11.1 billion in 1976 and to 50 billion barrels in 1995.

Almost overnight Mexico became a member of the exclusive group of oil-producing nations. Discoveries were swiftly exploited. In 1972, Mexico produced 300,000 barrels a day; by 1976 this figure had grown to 800,000 barrels a day. In 1997, Mexico pumped 3 million barrels per day, exporting 1.7 million of them.

The Mexican government was the beneficiary of the oil boom, for the constitution of 1917 granted rights to all domestic mineral deposits to the state. In theory, at least, the government would use the money from the sale and export of oil for improving its citizens' quality of life, but things did not turn out that way.

The oil discoveries coincided with price increases made by OPEC (Oil Producing and Exporting Countries) nations, among them Saudi Arabia, Kuwait, Nigeria, and Venezuela. OPEC doubled the cost of oil in 1972 and again in 1979. Mexico enjoyed an enormous windfall from this swift inflation of oil prices. Petroleum exports rose from 200,000 barrels a day in 1979 to 1 million barrels a day in early 1981. Buoyed by this good luck, the Mexican government borrowed money from foreign bankers and governments in a crash program to make Mexico a fully industrialized, developed country along the lines of a United States, Germany, or Japan. These dreams were never realized.

In failing to apply income from petroleum exports to the diversification of industry, the Mexican economy became increasingly oil-based, and as a result, more vulnerable. Oil's share of the country's total exports rose from 10 percent in 1976 to 75 percent in 1982. But in the spring of 1981, in the middle of Mexico's borrowing and spending spree, the price of oil began to drop. A worldwide economic recession reduced the demand for oil at the same time that more of it was being produced than ever before. Those two factors contributed to drastic reductions in price: From a high of $38 a barrel in early 1981, the amount paid for a barrel of oil plummeted, first to $34 a barrel in June 1981, then to around $25 a barrel a year later, and finally settling at around $15 a barrel for the rest of the 1980s.

This turn of events left Mexico out on an economic limb. In order to sustain its ambitious programs, it had to borrow even more heavily from foreign sources. In 1981, at the beginning of the economic crisis, the government borrowed $14.1 billion to prop up the economy. By 1993 it owed foreign banks and governments a staggering $118 billion. This debt gobbled up 40 percent of the money the country earned from exports. The interest on the debt alone amounted to more than $9 billion a year.

Mexico City stock exchange dealers place orders amid hectic trading in January 1996 as the Mexican economy begins to recover from economic crisis.

Despite repeated attempts to stabilize the economy by devaluing the peso and cutting government spending, Mexico's debt continued to rise, the value of its currency continued to fall, and its financial situation worsened. In early 1995, an emergency loan of $51 billion from the United States, the International Monetary Fund, and other organizations restored some confidence in Mexico's financial markets, but at a steep cost to the average Mexican, who saw government spending decrease by 10 percent, taxes rise, inflation increase to 40 percent, the gross domestic product shrink by more than 6 percent, and half a million jobs disappear.

In the midst of this economic crisis, the Mexican people began to discover that massive corruption and mismanagement had occurred during the oil boom. In 1980 alone, $130 million of Pemex money had disappeared because of "unexplained irregularities."

Although the economy began recovering in the late 1990s, the Mexican people, particularly the middle class and the poor, still reel under the burdens this disaster has placed on them. NAFTA's reduction of tariffs and the peso's weakness relative to the dollar have created a favorable climate for exports, and the maquiladoras have seen their production increase substantially. But wages for workers have declined. In 1994, for example, manufacturers spent $17.10 an hour for a worker in the United States, but only $2.61 for a Mexican worker. Mexican workers often do not make enough to purchase the goods they themselves produce. Dissatisfaction with these circumstances was one of the factors in the 1994 Zapatista revolt.

A young Mexican girl does stoop labor in a large tract of winter vegetables near Caliacan in the northern Mexican state of Sinaloa. The standard of living among many Mexican workers remains very low.

Communication and Transportation

With the development of mass media, the national government played a large role in controlling communications. It regulated both television and radio, and it authorized the production of programs on state-owned and private networks. Pro-government stories were encouraged, sometimes with bribes, and reports critical of the government were suppressed. The 1990s brought some relaxation of government controls, and the television industry began to experience both greater freedom and increased competition among broadcasters.

Today Mexico has 238 television stations and about 700 radio stations. There is a television set for every six and a half people. The telephone industry was sold to private investors in the early 1990s, and Mexico's notoriously inefficient telephone service saw a rapid improvement. The use of computers and e-mail has grown as a result.

The biggest and most influential newspapers in the country are published in Mexico City, including *Excelsior, La Reforma, La Jornada,* and *Uno Más Uno.* National news magazines such as *Proceso, Siempre,* and *Impacto* provide additional coverage. Like radio and television, print journalism has seen a surge in independent and nonpartisan reporting as government controls have loosened.

Good communications, trade, and tourism all depend on an adequate transportation system. In the late 19th and early 20th centuries, in order to take advantage of mining finds and later the discovery of oil reserves, the United States and Britain funded and built a railroad system that connected Mexico City with the United States and the Gulf of Mexico. After 1910, however, the level of construction decreased considerably. Not until the 1950s did Mexico have rail access to the Yucatán from Mexico City and a route west across Chihuahua and the Sierra Madre Occidental to the Pacific coast.

Just as a rail network made it easier for Mexico to trade with the United States, so have highways and airports spurred the tourist trade. Mexico's highways are modern and well constructed; the country has one of the most sophisticated highway systems in Latin America. The first major route, the Inter-American Highway, linking Mexico City with the United States at Laredo, Texas, opened in 1936. Today the country has 152,000 miles (254,000 kilometers) of roads, about half of which are paved. Traveling both highway and byway are 3.8 million commercial vehicles and 8 million private cars. In addition, there are two national airlines, and many charter airlines, and these and other international carriers fly into 83 airports throughout the country.

Mexican president Ernesto Zedillo addresses reporters at a White House press conference in Washington, D.C., with U.S. president Bill Clinton in 1995. The two men met to discuss the continuing economic crisis in Mexico.

8

Government and Society

Since 1929, Mexico has been governed by one giant authoritarian party, known as the Institutional Revolutionary party (or PRI, after the initials of its Spanish name, the Partido Revolucionario Institucional). Although the PRI has brought a measure of stability and economic and social advancement for many Mexicans, it has not encouraged a truly democratic spirit within the country. Only in recent years have other political parties been allowed to compete in meaningful ways with the PRI.

In the past, the PRI so thoroughly controlled all aspects of the country's economic, political, and social organization that it seldom lost an election. But the institutionalized corruption that produced this success caused such public outrage that the PRI itself enacted the electoral reforms that allowed its monopoly on power to be challenged. The presidential races of 1988 and 1994 were, by Mexican standards, close. And in 1997 the PRI lost its outright majority in the Chamber of Deputies.

The PRI and Its Challengers

The PRI was originally conceived to correct the great differences in wealth that existed between the classes in Mexico before the revolution. The constitution of 1917 promised many wonderful reforms. It guaranteed free public education for all as well as a free national health care program. The new government promised to take millions of acres of land from the great ranch owners and give them to the poor peasants. Workers would be permitted to form labor unions; an eight-hour workday and a minimum wage were guaranteed; and the constitution prohibited pay discrimination based on sex or nationality. Citizens could vote in honest elections. The new constitution promised all these things, but few of the promises were kept.

Instead a new political and social elite developed. The old criollo elite that had ruled Mexico since colonial times was forced to share its power. For the most part, Mexico's new elite was composed of mestizos who profited from the revolution of 1910.

The PRI does not resemble political parties found in most countries of the world. It is not a unified group with a clear-cut ideology and easily identifiable interests. Instead it is a sprawling organization with many different subgroups that compete for power within the party. Although it formally allows other political parties to compete in elections, until recently any genuine competition occurred within the PRI.

The PRI is powerful because of an unusual structure devised by party leaders, which reflects the competing special-interest groups in Mexico. Three basic organizations with strong ties to the PRI help the party control and steer politics within the country: the National Peasant Confederation (CNC), which represents peasants and small farmers; the Confederation of Mexican Workers (CTM), which represents the most important labor unions in the country; and the Confederation of Industrial Chambers (CONCAMIN), which represents industry and private enterprise.

These and other groups within the party exercise a voice in deciding which people will run as PRI candidates for major offices, including the governor's office in the different states and the offices of senator and deputy in the Congress. Most important of all,

The May Day Parade attracts nearly a million workers each year, who file past the National Palace in a display of union strength.

these groups influence the choice of the PRI candidate for president.

The president heads a huge government bureaucracy that controls virtually all aspects of Mexican life. Although limited to one six-year term, the president wields prodigious political power. For example, the president has great personal influence in deciding who can run for other offices—not only national and state offices, but also posts in municipal governments.

In such a system, the struggle for succession from one president to another is always a problem. Competition for power is carried out behind closed doors. So far the PRI has transferred power in a relatively smooth manner from one administration to another, but more and more ordinary Mexicans are beginning to feel that their interests are ignored under this system. As a result, in recent years other political parties in the country have offered stronger and stronger challenges to the PRI. The most prominent opposition parties are the National Action party (PAN), the Democratic Revo-

These farm workers have gathered to demand land that has been granted to them by the government but not yet released by the owner. The conflict over land rights sometimes leads to violence.

lutionary party (PRD), the Green Ecological party (PVEM), and the Workers party (PT).

The oldest and most powerful of these opposition groups is the National Action party. It is a relatively conservative party, representing business owners instead of workers. Its greatest strength is in the north and in urban centers, where rapid growth of industry has created a vigorous middle class. In 1988 the PAN won the

governorship of Baja California Norte. This was the first time since the emergence of the PRI that a governor had belonged to an opposition party. The number of such non-PRI officeholders continued to grow through the 1990s.

When Cuauhtémoc Cárdenas lost the contested 1988 presidential election, his supporters regrouped to form the PRD, which has become the most important leftist party in Mexico, comprising disaffected liberal members of the PRI and other, smaller leftist parties. It draws many of its leaders from the working classes, and it opposes government economic programs that tend to favor industries and exports at the expense of common laborers. It advocates political pluralism and liberalization. Though the PRD trailed both the PRI and the PAN in the 1994 national races, in 1997 Cárdenas became the first elected mayor of Mexico City—a post previously filled by presidential appointment.

The Military and the Police

For many years after winning its independence, Mexico was at the mercy of military strongmen who assumed political power. These military leaders were known as *caudillos*. Often the caudillo who could gather the strongest army emerged as president of the country. This caused great political instability, and few leaders had the opportunity to serve out their entire terms of office, much less to establish a program of economic or social development that would be pursued by succeeding administrations.

In the 1920s, after the revolution, presidents Obregón and Calles (both former generals) drastically trimmed the size of the army and bought off rival military leaders with large grants of land. The legendary Pancho Villa, probably the most famous general of the Mexican Revolution, was bought off in this way. Villa was given a ranch in the state of Chihuahua, where he raised chickpeas for several years until he was assassinated in 1923.

Today, Mexico has an active military of 175,000. The government exercises direct control over the army and carefully rotates command so that no army leader builds up an independent following outside the party. By taming the army, the government has taken a great step toward achieving political tranquillity in Mexico.

Police powers in Mexico are handled by a variety of federal, state, and local police departments. The most powerful of these is the Federal Judicial Police, most commonly known as the Federales. The Federales are charged with keeping tabs on all criminal activity in Mexico. They have been active in the recent U.S.-Mexican drive against the cultivation and sale of illegal drugs, and they also are supposed to ensure that none of the other police groups in Mexico engages in corrupt practices.

In fact, however, elements within the Federales and most of the other police organizations engage in systematic corruption. Though some law-enforcement officials have been murdered by drug traffickers, many members of the various police forces routinely take bribes in exchange for allowing the unimpeded flow of contraband. The practice is so common in Mexico that a nickname for it has made its way into Mexican Spanish. The bribe is called *la mordita*, the "little bite."

Most Mexicans greatly resent police corruption, and the city police are so regularly booed at the Independence Day parade in Mexico City that they have to turn their sirens on to drown out the catcalls.

Education

The constitution of 1917 guaranteed free public education in Mexico. In the first decade following the revolution, the government built thousands of new schools, particularly in rural areas. Today the government requires children to attend school from ages 6 through 18. Most children do receive several years of schooling.

On the average, Mexican children receive five to six years of schooling, but the adult literacy rate is high and college enrollments are up.

But according to estimates, only about 59 percent of children between 6 and 18 are actually enrolled in school at any one time; of these, about three-quarters are elementary students. Low attendance in secondary education is particularly common in poor communities, where the schools are few and far apart and where older children generally need to help support their families.

Both elementary and secondary schools teach varied academic subjects such as art, social science, natural science, math, and lan-

guages. But because Mexico needs more skilled workers and technicians in agriculture and industry, the government has increased the number of vocational and technical training programs.

Mexico has more than 80 colleges, with over 1.2 million students. The government requires students who graduate from public universities to perform some form of social service related to their field.

Since 1960, the government has made a particular effort to wipe out illiteracy in adults. In 1985 the state reorganized its education system, making literacy the primary goal. Since 1960, officials estimate, adult illiteracy has fallen from 29 percent to 10 percent; this means that 90 percent of all adults can read and write.

Health and Health Care

Like their liberal arts counterparts, all medical students have a social service requirement. They must practice in rural communities in order to obtain a medical degree.

The health care system in Mexico is very complex. Some people see private doctors, while others get medical care through special institutions connected with their employment. Separate institutions serve workers at state-owned companies, and there are additional health services for the armed forces. People not eligible for any of these may be served by hospitals and clinics run by the Secretariat of Health.

But many poor Mexicans, who remain outside the system of health services that the government provides, receive no professional medical care. In the mid-1990s, the government began efforts to coordinate the different branches of the health care system, in part to deal with the more than 50,000 Mexicans who contract tuberculosis each year.

Dysentery, typhoid, malaria, polio, and the measles once claimed victims regularly in Mexico, but the government has greatly reduced their frequency through inoculations and sanitation programs. A vigorous insecticide program has decreased the numbers of the deadly tropical-zone mosquitoes that transmit malaria. These efforts have helped lower the infant mortality rate, which now stands at 25 deaths per 1,000 live births (this means that 25 of every 1,000 infants will die during their first year).

Acquired immunodeficiency syndrome (AIDS) is becoming a large concern in the country, with more than 22,000 cases reported by 1995. Since this number does not include unreported cases or those people with HIV, the virus that causes AIDS, Mexico, like other countries, faces increasing burdens of education, prevention, and treatment.

Malnourishment affects 40 percent of all Mexicans, while malnutrition is a serious problem among the poorest 20 percent of the population, affecting children especially. Malnutrition in Mexico results from a lack of food, not from its poor quality. The peasant diet is in fact a healthy one, consisting mostly of corn tortillas and beans, which are both excellent sources of protein. The corn is cooked in lime, which provides minerals, and the beans are cooked with chili peppers and tomatoes, which provide vitamins. Most people are too poor to afford meat. Thus the peasant diet is low in salt, fat, and sugar. The only problem is that there is often simply not enough food to go around.

Housing for much of the population is also substandard, with as many as 20 million people living in homes with dirt floors and no plumbing. Housing and nutrition both suffer because of the lack of regular jobs for many people. The official unemployment rate in the mid-1990s was under 10 percent, but many observers believe that the true figure is considerably higher. Perhaps 40 percent of the work force can be considered unemployed or underemployed.

A Native American mother and daughter sell embroidery in the market at San Miguel de Allende.

9

Today and Tomorrow

Mexico is a deeply troubled nation. It has inherited political authoritarianism and economic inequality from its turbulent past. Yet its people are hardworking and imaginative. Its future success depends on the way it tackles three major concerns: the economy, the rising population, and the challenge of the one-party rule of the PRI.

Mexico needs to get itself out from under the heavy burden of debt that has weighed down its economy since the early 1980s. It must continue to diversify its economy, create new jobs, and modernize its agricultural sector. The advantages that oil production and NAFTA have brought to financial markets and industries need to be shared among all Mexicans. This is the greatest challenge for the economy and the society: to reduce the unequal distribution of wealth between the rich and the poor.

These problems might be impossible to solve unless Mexico lowers its birthrate. Between 1940 and 1970, Mexico's population growth rate jumped from 1.1 percent a year to 3.5 percent a year, and its population grew by 150 percent, from 20 million to 50 million people. By 1996 the annual increase in population had fallen to 1.8

Workers attend a rally in support of Cuauhtémoc Cárdenas, the presidential candidate who opposed the PRI. Greater political freedom for Mexicans seems inevitable.

percent a year, but even at this lower rate, Mexico can expect to have a population of approximately 120 million people by the year 2010. A larger population means the government will have to work harder to provide new housing, jobs, and social services.

Finally there appears to be a link between Mexico's social and economic problems and the crisis of political expression. The one-party rule imposed by the PRI for most of the 20th century does not serve the needs of modern Mexico. Mexicans became especially outspoken in the 1980s and 1990s about the faults of their political system. For the first time since the PRI was created, real political challenges have been offered by other political parties. The conservative National Action party (PAN) and the liberal Democratic Revolutionary party (PRD) have mounted major drives against the PRI in the last decade. As a result, the PRI has lost the governorships of several states, the mayoralty of the world's largest city, and its majority in the Chamber of Deputies. By 1997, more than 40 percent of the population was governed, at the state or local level, by opposition officeholders. Though the PRI is still by far the dominant party in Mexican politics, the pluralization of the political system represented by the PRI's recent losses may signal a long-term gain for Mexican democracy.

There is no way of telling how, when, or if Mexico's problems will be solved. In the meanwhile, the lament attributed to President Porfirio Díaz still applies today. "Poor Mexico," the president is said to have declared, "so far from God and so close to the United States."

GLOSSARY

castillo   A large fireworks construction that is traditional at Mexican fiestas.

caudillo   A military strongman who assumes political power and controls the affairs of a region or country.

conquistador   One of the Spanish soldiers who came to the Americas to engage in military conquest for the purpose of enriching himself.

criollo   A person of European descent living in Mexico.

federal   A member of the Federal Judicial Police, the national police force of Mexico.

frijol   A bean, often the pinto, black, or red bean, that is one of the staples of the Mexican diet.

huipil   A brightly colored, rectangular dress often worn by Native American Mexican women.

katún   A Mayan unit of time equal to 20 years.

mestizo   A person of mixed European and Native American descent.

milagro   An object, sometimes in the shape of a heart, arm, leg, head, or other part of the body, pinned to the altar of a church to give thanks to Jesus or the Virgin Mary in return for the cure of an ailment.

la mordita	The "little bite," a routine bribe paid by Mexican citizens to police officers.
NAFTA	The North American Free Trade Agreement, established by Mexico, Canada, and the United States in 1994 to gradually eliminate most tariffs on imports and exports among the three countries.
poncho	A cape, used to ward off rain or cold, often worn by Mexican men.
rebozo	A shawl worn by Mexican women.
Sierra Madres	The "mother mountains," or the main mountain ranges of Mexico.
sombrero	A hat worn by men in Mexico.
tamal	A long, thin cornmeal roll, stuffed with meat or chicken and baked or fried.
tierra caliente	The hot land, found at low elevation in the tropical latitudes.
tierra fría	The cold land, found in Mexico on the northern plateau and at the highest mountaintop elevations.
tierra templada	The temperate land, found at moderate elevations in the tropical latitudes.
tortilla	A thin pancake, often made of cornmeal, commonly used in Mexican cooking.
vaquero	A Mexican cowboy.

INDEX

125

W

Workers party, 111

Y

Yucatán, 29, 30, 31, 32, 80, 100, 104
Yucatán Peninsula, 23, 30, 39, 47, 100

Z

Zacatecas, 95
Zapata, Emiliano, 59, 60, 65
Zapatista Army of National Liberation, 32, 65, 103
Zapotecs, 29, 30, 56
Zedillo, Ernesto, 65

PICTURE CREDITS

AP/Wide World Photos: pp. 2, 16–17, 28, 64, 71, 74, 103, 110–11; Art Resource: p. 14; Steve Benbow/Woodfin Camp and Associates: p. 88; The Bettmann Archive: p. 23; John Curtis/Taurus Photos: p. 87 (top); Courtesy Department Library Services, American Museum of Natural History: p. 37 (neg. # 286823), pp. 44–45 (neg. # 292759), p. 53 (neg. # 286821); Charles Marden Fitch/Taurus Photos: pp. 20, 72, 92; Yann Gamblin/UNICEF: p. 63; Kenneth Garrett/Woodfin Camp and Associates: p. 85 (top); Gaworski/Taurus Photos: pp. 30–31; Giraudon/Art Resource: p. 54; Spencer C. Grant III/Taurus Photos: pp. 26–27, 66, 76; Ellis Herwig/Taurus Photos: p. 82; Instituto Nacional de las Bellas Artes de Mexico/Art Resource: p. 90; Eric Kroll/ Taurus Photos: pp. 86–87; Library of Congress: pp. 48, 57, 58, 60–61, 95, 96–97, 99; Logan/Courtesy Department Library Services, American Museum of Natural History: p. 51 (neg. # 329237), p. 52 (neg. # 392241): Lowenfish/Courtesy Department Library Services, American Museum of Natural History: p. 38 (neg. # 330375), p. 41 (neg. # 330359); Owen C. Luck/Taurus Photos: pp. 86, 114–15; Phil Mezey/Taurus Photos: pp. 69, 118; Kal Muller/Woodfin Camp and Associates: pp. 81, 83 (bottom); Karen R. Preuss/Taurus Photos: p. 79; Scott Ransom/Taurus Photos: p. 84 (top); Reuter/Bettmann Archive: pp. 109, 120; Reuters/Heriberto Rodriguez/Archive Photos, p. 102; Reuters/Win McNamee/Archive Photos, p. 106; L. L. T. Rhodes/Taurus Photos: pp. 84–85; Rota/Courtesy Department Library Services, American Museum of Natural History: p. 34 (neg. # 321216), p. 46 (neg. # 326597); Barry Schreibman/ Taurus Photos: pp. 82–83